Southern Lighthouses

SOUTHERN LIGHTHOUSES

Chesapeake Bay to the Gulf of Mexico

Photographs by Bruce Roberts
Text by Ray Jones

Globe Pequot Press

Chester, Connecticut

Library of Congress Cataloging-in-Publication Data

Roberts, Bruce, 1930-
    Southern lighthouses / photographs by Bruce Roberts : text by Ray Jones — 1st ed.
      p. cm.
    Bibliography: p.
    Includes index.
    ISBN 0–87106–548-7
    1. Lighthouses—Southern States. I. Jones, Ray, 1948- .II. Title.
  VK1024.S66R63 1989
  387.1'55—dc20
                                                         89–32601
                                                         CIP

Manufactured in the United States of America
First Edition/Second Printing

To the memory of lighthouse keeper Harry Claiborne and all the other brave men and women who, throughout history, have kept the lights burning.

CONTENTS

Biloxi Lighthouse, Mississippi

INTRODUCTION

History's first great lighthouse was also its tallest. Built in about 280 B.C. on an island in the bustling harbor of Alexandria, the Pharos tower reached 450 feet into the skies of ancient Egypt. Its light, produced by a fire kept blazing on its roof, could probably be seen from up to twenty-nine miles out in the Mediterranean. Mariners needed the Pharos Light because Alexandria stood on the flat Nile Delta, and there were no mountains or other natural features to help them find the city.

Ancient peoples had long made a practice of banking fires on hills and mountainsides to bring their sailors home from the sea. With its artificial mountain, Alexandria pulled in seamen from the entire known world. The delta city became the busiest and most prosperous port in the world, and it remained so for almost 1,000 years. Trading ships from Greece, Carthage, and Rome flocked to the city's wharves to load up with the grain grown in wondrous abundance in fields along the banks of the Nile. The sight of the Pharos light burning far up near the dome of the sky must have filled the breasts of countless sea captains with awe.

The American South also has a proud city named Alexandria, and it, too, is a port. Like the first Alexandria, it was once the heart of a rich agricultural region. Today, it is a wealthy suburb, located just across the Potomac from the nation's capital. In fact, Alexandria was included within the original boundaries of the District of Columbia, but its citizens preferred to cast their lot with agrarian Virginia. At Alexandria's Jones Point, some five or six miles down the Potomac from the city of Washington, is a stone marking one of the corners of the old, ten-mile-square federal district.

Also at Jones Point stands a small, rectangular building with whitewashed wooden walls, a pitched roof, and a porch. Probably no more than twenty feet high, its appearance suggests a nineteenth-century country schoolhouse. Except for the tiny lantern protruding from its roof, one might never guess that it had anything in common with the Pharos tower of ancient Alexandria. But it does. It is a lighthouse.

Although it has been inactive for decades, the Jones Point Light guided ships into Alexandria, Washington, and Georgetown for more than half a century. Built in 1855, it can now claim distinction as the nation's oldest standing inland lighthouse. In counterpoint to its gargantuan ancestor in Egypt, it is also among the world's smallest lighthouses.

The South has many other lighthouses, some much older than the Jones Point Light. While none reach the extraordinary height of the ancient Pharos Tower, many of them are very tall indeed. Built on flat, mostly featureless headlands, they have to be tall to serve effectively as sea marks. The Pensacola Lighthouse rises 160 feet above the Florida sand; the Cape Charles Light in Virginia stands 180 feet above the water; and the Hatteras Tower, the tallest brick lighthouse in America, soars 193 feet above the Outer Banks.

Ptolemy Soter erected this marble watchtower, or lighthouse, on the island of Pharos near the Port of Alexandria, Egypt. (This engraving appeared in A Complete Collection of Voyages and Travels *(London, 1744-48, vol. 1) by John Harris. Photo courtesy Department of Rare Books, William R. Perkins Library, Duke University)*

Although it has long been inactive, the Jones Point Light is the nation's oldest standing lighthouse.

Lighthouses have always been a source of intense fascination for landlubbers as well as sailors. Not only are they interesting as architectural achievements, but penetrating the darkness with their lights, they offer direction—to ships and to the human spirit. No less than for the captain of a Roman grain ship approaching Alexandria's Pharos, our first glimpse of one of the South's towering lighthouses—or even of a midget such as the Jones Point Light—is likely to fill us with wonder.

Lighthouses are always interesting, and each, in its own way, is beautiful. Of course, some are lovelier or can boast more exciting pasts than others. Although quite broad in scope, this book does not attempt to picture or tell the story of every one of the South's many coastal lights. Instead, it focuses on lighthouses of special architectural or historical significance.

Many would say the South's most famous and impressive lighthouse stands on North Carolina's Cape Hatteras. In the following passage, photographer Bruce Roberts (who shot the photographs for this book) describes his first encounter with this giant.

A GIANT STANDS ON LIQUID SAND

My first glimpse of the Cape Hatteras Lighthouse came on a cold winter afternoon in 1961. Crossing the bridge over Oregon Inlet where Pamlico Sound meets the Atlantic Ocean, I drove south over forty miles of rough, narrow road. Warned by the signs posted along the road, I knew that if I hooked a wheel off the pavement, I was in trouble. The sands on Hatteras are almost as liquid as its surf, and an unwary driver can easily bury all four wheels down to the axles. But I was cautious and reached Cape Hatteras safely.

On the drive down, I had not passed another car nor seen another person, and at the cape, I was completely alone except for the old, silent lighthouse itself. Cape Hatteras is separated from the North Carolina mainland by the thirty-mile-wide Pamlico Sound, so if you are alone there, you are really alone. At Hatteras, it's easy to empathize with the lonely sailors who for centuries have passed by the cape and struggled to avoid its shoals.

The Cape Hatteras Lighthouse stands on the outer rim of the North American continent, marking an uncertain boundary between land and sea. Watching the waves pound the beach, it becomes obvious that the land has only a tenuous hold on this place and may have to give it back to the sea at any time. But the ocean's grip on its own domain is also slippery. Reaching from Hatteras several miles out into the Atlantic, the Diamond Shoals are almost as much a part of the land as of the sea. These treacherous shoals are very shallow and have punctured and torn open the hulls of countless ships. The shoals are, in fact, one of the reasons a lighthouse was built here.

The Hatteras Light has saved many ships, though there are some it has not

saved. On the shifting, sandy ocean bottom beyond the cape rest Spanish galleons, which over the centuries have spilled out caches of silver and gold doubloons into the sea. Nearby are the rusting decks of German U-boats and the twisted hulks of British tankers sunk by torpedoes. Further offshore is the final resting place of the *Monitor,* which sank while being towed past the cape. The Civil War ironclad, nemesis of the Confederate warship *Virginia,* sits upright on the bottom, its single turret still intact.

A lifeboat tossed up on the sand by the sea is a reminder of the many shipwrecks and lives lost off Cape Hatteras in years gone by. It is likely that this lifeboat came off a tanker sunk by a German submarine during World War II.

During World War II, a destroyer mistook the *Monitor* for a German submarine and dropped depth charges on the wreck.

Extinguished by the war, the Cape Hatteras Light was temporarily dark when the *Monitor* sank in 1862, and it was dark now as I got out of my car and walked over the dunes toward the tower. I had come to the Outer Banks on a photography assignment, and I wanted a picture of Hatteras Lighthouse with its light burning. To me, a lighthouse without its light is asleep, or worse, it's a dead thing; it's not a lighthouse at all, but rather a "darkhouse." The Hatteras light is automated; it comes on every evening as night approaches. So all I had to do was set up my tripod, ready my camera, and wait for the daylight to fade. Soon, the light would flash on in the lantern almost 200 feet above the sea.

Years ago, the light in the Hatteras tower was focused by a big Fresnel lens imported from France. The lens was made in Paris, its huge glass prisms polished by the hands of orphans and homeless street people. These destitute workers were paid only a few pennies a day to polish the three-sided prisms and the round bulls-eye in the center of the lens. Although manufactured under sweatshop conditions, the Fresnel lenses were a godsend to lighthouse keepers and the mariners they served. Truly ingenious inventions, they could gather up and concentrate every flicker from a whale-oil lamp.

Fresnels came in a hierarchy of sizes, referred to as first-order, second-order, third-order, and so on. Among the standard Fresnels, the first-order lenses were the largest, with an inside diameter of roughly six feet. The smallest were the sixth-order lenses, with an inside diameter of only about one foot. The Hatteras Fresnel was a powerful first-order lens able to project a tightly focused beam of light that could be seen from twenty miles at sea.

But the old Fresnel was now gone. It had been replaced by a more modern light source—an aerobeacon with a 1,000-watt lamp. How appropriate to have an airport beacon in a lighthouse so close to Kitty Hawk, a few dozen miles to the north. Orville and Wilbur Wright would have approved.

At last the darkness came, and the automatic beacon switched on, making its first revolution of the night. A few moments later, I took my first picture of the lighthouse flashing out its message just as it had for almost 160 years. Sailors read the message as a warning: "This is Hatteras—stay clear!"

North of Hatteras is Jockey's Ridge, a huge sand dune looking down on the town of Nags Head. The unusual names of the town and the big dune are reminders that not all guiding lights are trustworthy. It is said that the infamous "Blackbeard" and other pirates tied lanterns to the necks of horses and walked the animals along the crest of the ridge. To sailors at sea, the lanterns seemed to bob up and down like cabin lights on a ship riding the waves. This evil trick lured many unsuspecting captains too close to the shore, where their ships were trapped in the shallows and became easy prey for the pirates. Unfortunately, treachery of this kind has been common throughout history.

Today, however, sailors know they can trust the navigational beacons that shine from our coasts. The Hatteras Light has guided countless thousands of ships safely past the protruding cape and its dangerous Diamond Shoals. Ironically, the lighthouse itself may not be safe. I have photographed the Hatteras Light many times since my first lonely night on the cape, and each time I've visited with my camera, it has seemed to me that the sea has moved closer to the old tower. The waves have been eating up the beach, and soon the ocean may threaten the foundation of the lighthouse.

This is not the first time that the ocean has closed in on the lighthouse. But always in the past, just when the waves seemed about to consume the tower, the water backed away. Now the sea approaches again. Where will it stop this time? In 1987 the National Park Service drew up a plan to mount the 208-foot, 2,800-ton structure on steel rails and move it back from the sea. If that ever happens, I hope to be there to photograph it.

CHAPTER ONE

LIGHTS OF
THE LIBERTY CAPES

Maryland and Virginia

Lights of The Liberty Capes

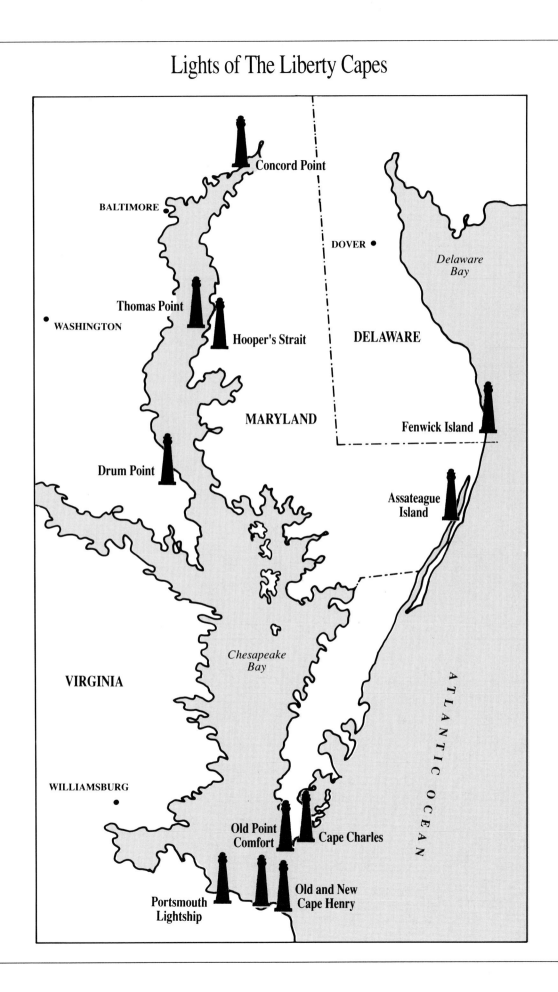

In 1718 Alexander Spotswood, the governor of colonial Virginia, approached the British Board of Trade with a remarkable idea. Why not build a tower on Cape Henry at the mouth of the Chesapeake and place a light atop it to guide ships into the bay? Just such a tower had been built a couple of years before in Massachusetts, and almost overnight, Boston Harbor had become a magnet for sea trade. Spotswood was certain that a similar structure erected on one of the Virginia capes would make the Chesapeake safer for shipping and greatly increase commerce in the region. Spotswood told the British that the benefits of the project seemed to him "so obvious that I have often wondered why so useful a work has not been undertaken long ere now."

The Board of Trade listened politely to the governor's proposal and then proceeded to ignore it. The British government had begun to grow suspicious and, perhaps, a touch envious of the swelling prosperity of its colonies in America. Parliament had no intention of spending good British sterling on a project likely to help the business-minded American colonists make still more money. So the British built no lighthouse on Cape Henry. Three-quarters of a century later, General Charles Cornwallis may have wished they had.

By the mid-1770s British subjects in the American colonies were fed up with their mother country. They hated paying taxes—even a penny a pound on tea—and the negligent attitude of British officials toward needed public projects, such as building lighthouses, made them even more obstinate about opening their purses for the king. It seemed to the colonists that His Majesty George III considered them a lot of country bumpkins. Feeling they were being treated like second-class citizens, increasing numbers of Americans were reaching the conclusion that they must take their destinies into their own hands.

Caught up in the independent spirit sweeping the colonies, the people of Virginia and Maryland decided to pool their resources and build their own lighthouse on Cape Henry. In their view, if the project were left entirely to the British, the mouth of the Chesapeake would be dark forever. But work on the lighthouse had barely started when the alienation of Americans boiled over into open rebellion, and the effort had to be abandoned. Instead of constructing a lighthouse, the colonists now undertook to build a new nation.

By August 1781, when General Cornwallis marched his redcoat army into Yorktown, the British had been fighting for five long years to put down the American revolt. Weary of the struggle, they had sent Cornwallis to America with orders to bring the war to a speedy conclusion. Tough and ruthless, Cornwallis had no scruples at all about burning people's homes and crops and driving off their livestock. He was sent to America to heap misery on the king's unruly subjects, and in a series of destructive sweeps through the Carolinas and Virginia during the spring and summer of 1781, that is exactly what he did. Believing smugly that he had brought the revolutionaries to their knees, Cornwallis then fell back to rest and resupply his troops at Yorktown, a small port located conveniently on the banks of the York River near the point where it flows into the Chesapeake.

Cornwallis had one important flaw as a commander—an arrogant disregard for the military prowess of his opponents. He had little respect for the fighting abilities of the French, who had entered the war on the side of the Americans, and even less for George Washington and his ragtag Continental Army. So, even with his back to the York River and the Chesapeake beyond, Cornwallis felt perfectly safe at Yorktown. Indeed, he was so confident that he neglected to hurry his soldiers in their task of fortifying his new base of operations.

It must have astounded the British general to learn, as he did in mid-September, that Washington's army was closing in on Yorktown. Marching alongside the Virginia planter and his Continentals was a large body of French infantry as well as a second American army under Lafayette. Cornwallis realized with a start that he would soon be dangerously outnumbered.

But the general remained calm. He knew he had a resource near at hand that the Americans could not hope to match—the British navy. He had every reason to believe that a fleet of friendly ships would soon appear and, with their massed cannons, send his enemies fleeing into the woods. Cornwallis felt sure that, at the very least, he could count on the Royal Navy to help evacuate his troops.

Exactly as Cornwallis thought, help was on the way; a large British squadron of twenty-seven ships commanded by Admiral Thomas Graves was pushing south under full sail. But the relief squadron never reached Yorktown. Just as Graves cut westward into the Chesapeake at the Virginia Capes, he slammed into an unexpected obstacle: A powerful fleet of thirty-six French warships under Rear Admiral de Grasse blocked the way. Cannons flashed and thundered for hour after hour, and when the battle was over, three British fighting ships had been sunk and the rest were fleeing north in disorder.

Cornwallis's proud redcoats now found themselves tightly squeezed between the Americans and French to their front and the York River at their backs. The British crouched low in their trenches as cannonballs rained in from several directions. The artillery barrage became so fierce that Cornwallis had to move his headquarters into a cave under the bluffs along the Yorktown waterfront. To prevent French ships from sailing into the harbor and shelling him from the rear, Cornwallis created artificial shoals in the river by scuttling his supply boats.

The British fought on for weeks, but with no help coming from beyond the capes, the outcome of the siege was no longer in question. On October 20 a band played a tune called "The World Turned Upside Down," as the redcoats marched out from behind their fortifications and surrendered. The Americans had won the Revolutionary War and with it the right to collect their own taxes and, if they wished, build their own lighthouses.

What course might history have taken if the British had built a lighthouse on the Virginia Capes shortly after 1718, when the colonists first asked for it? Had the British been more solicitous of their colonies, paid closer attention to their needs, maybe there would never have been a revolution in the first place. And even if the split was inevitable, the battle of Yorktown and the war itself might have ended differently. Perhaps a light on Cape Henry would have enabled a relief fleet to slip past the French blockade in the night and rescue Cornwallis.

BY THE DAWN'S EARLY LIGHT

Roughly a dozen years after the Yorktown siege, the United States government built a lighthouse on Cape Henry, the very place where old Governor Spotswood had envisioned a tower and light a lifetime earlier (Spotswood died in 1740). Its fish-oil lamps were first lit one night in October 1792 and were still burning brightly some twenty years later, when British warships returned to the Chesapeake to fight the War of 1812. This time the Royal Navy met far less opposition at the capes than it had in 1781. In fact, the British captains may very well have used the Cape Henry beacon to help them steer their ships into the bay.

The invaders remained in the Chesapeake for more than a year, slamming the door on commerce and terrorizing the population. As the British burned and blasted one bay-side community after another, the Americans fought back bravely but ineffectively with a pitiful array of clumsy barges on which they had mounted field cannon. At Hampton Roads, the British captured Fort Monroe, using as a watchtower the Old Point Comfort Lighthouse, which had been in service for only about a dozen years.

Eventually, the redcoats attacked the city of Washington itself, setting fire to the Capitol and the White House. At Baltimore, the British tried an unsuccessful military experiment, bombing Fort McHenry with rockets launched from small boats in the harbor. Most of the rockets exploded high in the air before they ever reached the fort. The British failed to capture the fort, but the sight of the rockets exploding like fireworks over Fort McHenry inspired Francis Scott Key to write a poem—"Oh, say, can you see . . ."

IRON CLASHES WITH IRON

Almost half a century after Key penned his famous lines, war again swept over the Chesapeake. This time it was a great Civil War, with American fighting American, North against South. Vastly inferior to the Northern side in naval strength, the Southerners were no friends of lighthouses. To make navigation as difficult as possible for Union sailors, the Confederates snuffed out all but a handful of the lights from Virginia all the way to the Mexican border. The Cape Henry Light was extinguished in 1861, the first year of the struggle. It remained dark in 1862, when the Confederates made their boldest attempt to punch a hole in the tight Union naval blockade of the Southern coasts.

On the morning of March 8, 1862, the Confederate States Ship *Virginia* steamed out of the James River and bore down on a squadron of Union frigates anchored in the Chesapeake within sight of the Old Port Comfort Lighthouse at Fort Monroe. Encased in a shell of iron plates two inches thick, the *Virginia* was a fighting ship such as the world had never seen.

Until this strange vessel appeared from around a bend in the James, sailors on the Union frigate *Cumberland* had been doing laundry and hanging their wet uniforms in the rigging to dry in the breeze. They had reason to be relaxed; as far as they knew, the South had no real navy. The last thing they expected was an attack, but incredibly, an attack was coming. There, in plain sight, was the *Virginia* lumbering along at its sluggish top speed of five knots directly toward the *Cumberland*.

The laundry was snatched down out of the rigging, and the crew quickly readied the frigate's guns. The *Cumberland* started firing while the *Virginia* was still three-quarters of a mile away. But to their horror, the gunners on the doomed frigate saw their shots bounce harmlessly off the *Virginia's* thick armor. They reloaded and fired, reloaded and fired, but there was no stopping the *Virginia*. It kept plowing forward until, with a tremendous shock, it drove a 1,500-pound iron ram into the wooden ribs of the *Cumberland*. Mortally wounded, the Union ship went down swiftly, taking much of her crew with her.

That same day, the *Virginia* also destroyed the frigate *Congress* and drove several other Union vessels aground on the spreading Chesapeake mud flats. Then, with night approaching, the Southerners took their seemingly invincible ship back to the James. But on the following day, they brought the *Virginia* out again, meaning to put an end to the Union blockade once and for all. This time, however, there was a surprise waiting for the Confederates. Directly in the path of the *Virginia* lay a low, turreted vessel described by one astonished Southern sailor as "a cheese box on a raft." But this small ship, its deck continuously washed over by the waves, was no joke. It was, in fact, an ironclad like the *Virginia,* part of a whole new class of fighting ships called "Monitors."

The *Virginia* and the *Monitor* pounded away at one another for hours, but to little effect. Their historic confrontation ended in a draw. Neither would ever be defeated in battle, though within a few months, both would be sunk. The *Virginia* was scuttled by its own crew to keep it from falling into the hands of Union troops who had overrun the Confederate naval yard at Norfolk. The *Monitor* sank in a fierce storm only a few miles south of the Hatteras Lighthouse.

U-BOATS OFF THE CAPES

The Civil War clash of ironclads was not the last time ships would fight near the Virginia Capes. Many times between 1942 and 1945, the keepers of the Cape Henry Lighthouse saw flashes in the night and heard the thunder of exploding torpedoes fired by German submarines. Despite heavy patrolling by the Coast Guard and U.S. Navy destroyers, U-boat "wolf packs" often lurked in the waters beyond the capes.

The wolves were especially hungry during the winter and spring of 1942. On January 30 of that year, the tanker *Rochester* received a torpedo amidships and sank within sight of the Cape Henry Light. Two weeks later, a pair of torpedoes took down the tanker *E. H. Blum,* also near Cape Henry. On March 20 a German submarine sank the tanker *Oakmar.* In April the tankers *David Atwater* and *Tiger* and the freighters *Robin Hood* and *Alcoa Skipper* were all sent to the bottom by U-boats.

The carnage continued at intervals throughout World War II. The Cape Henry keepers would see a flash or hear a rumble and know that yet another vessel had fallen prey to the unseen enemy beneath the waves. There was little the keepers could do but watch, lend life-saving assistance if they could, and keep their light burning.

THOMAS POINT LIGHT
Chesapeake Bay, Maryland - 1825

The growth of shipping on the Chesapeake convinced the government to build a small tower on Thomas Point not far from Annapolis. A bank of treacherous shoals extending out into the Chesapeake forced vessels requiring deep water to swing wide around the point. Obviously, a light was needed to help them keep their distance at night. In 1824 federal officials bought seven acres on the point for about $500 and hired a novice contractor named John Donohoo to construct a small tower for about $5,600. The inexperienced Donohoo did a poor job of building the tower, however, and a few years later it had to be torn down and rebuilt.

The contract for reconstruction of the Thomas Point Lighthouse went to Winslow Lewis, who held a patent on the "reflecting and magnifying" lantern used in many American lighthouses (Lewis's system was eventually shown to be inadequate and was replaced in most lighthouses by high-quality Fresnel lenses). Lewis rebuilt the lighthouse for only about $2,500, and his tower guarded the point for more than thirty years. But its light was weak, and Chesapeake sailors grumbled that it was "utterly useless" in fog or foul weather.

In 1875 the Lighthouse Board decided to move the light offshore and place it where it would be most effective—out in the bay, immediately over the shoals. The new lighthouse was a small hexagon-shaped building perched on screw piles.

Abandoned, the Lewis tower on the point eventually collapsed, but for more than a century, the light on the shoals has weathered storms, floods, and ice floes— everything that nature has thrown at it. The Thomas Point Light remains active.

The only way to see this lighthouse is by boat. Annapolis, Maryland, is the nearest port. For possible sight-seeing boat tours, contact the Tourism Council of Annapolis and Anne Arundel County, Six Dock Street, Annapolis, Maryland 21401; (301) 280–0445.

The Thomas Point Light remains on the shoals of Chesapeake Bay, where it has stood since 1875.

CONCORD POINT LIGHT
Havre de Grace, Maryland - 1827

Two years after he had built the Thomas Point Lighthouse—and botched the job—John Donohoo won a contract to erect a lighthouse on Concord Point at Havre de Grace. Donohoo completed the thirty-two-foot stone tower in less than a year for $3,500, and this time his work was solid. The tower still stands today, looking very much as it did when its lamps were first lit in 1827.

Originally, the lantern held a set of lamps and sixteen-inch reflectors. Later, these were exchanged for a fifth-order Fresnel lens, among the smallest Fresnels available. Today, the tower displays a fixed green light as a private aid to navigation. It has been automated since the 1920s.

All the keepers of the Havre de Grace Light came from a single family, that of war hero John O'Niel. During the War of 1812, O'Niel had made a quixotic one-man stand against an entire British fleet. Miraculously, he survived and later was rewarded with the post of keeper at the Havre de Grace Light. The job was passed down from one generation of O'Niels to the next. Finally, in the 1920s, the light was automated, and great-grandson Harry O'Niel had to surrender the tower key.

Take State 155 off I-95 into Havre de Grace and turn left onto Otsego Street. Then turn right onto Saint John's Street and, finally, left again at the sign for Concord Point. If you get lost, remember that the light is near the Susquehanna River in the southeast part of town.

The lighthouse is open for tours every Sunday afternoon from May to October. For more information, contact the Friends of Concord Point Lighthouse, Box 212, Havre de Grace, Maryland 21078; (301) 939-1340 or (301) 939–2016.

The thirty-two-foot stone tower on Concord Point was completed at a cost of $3,500—in 1827.
(Photo by Hans Gunder)

FENWICK ISLAND LIGHT
Fenwick Island, Delaware - 1858

Actually, the Fenwick Island Light is in Delaware, but since the Mason-Dixon Line runs right through the lighthouse property, the tower can be viewed without ever leaving Maryland. In fact, Mr. Mason and Mr. Dixon began their famous survey on Fenwick Island. Landing on the island in 1750, they drove a stake beside a grove of mulberry trees and extended their survey line to the west from that point. Today, the white lighthouse tower stands beside the very spot where Mason and Dixon drove their stake.

Built in 1858 to guide ships into the Delaware Bay, the Fenwick Island Lighthouse is eighty-three feet tall and holds a third-order Fresnel lens. The light, visible from fifteen miles at sea, fills an otherwise dark gap between the Assateague Light in Virginia and the Cape Henlopen Light to the north.

The lighthouse stands in a trailer park on the west side of Route 1 near the intersection of Highway 54. It is located just across the Delaware state line from Maryland and just south of Bethany Beach and Fenwick Island State Park. The tower is open by appointment. Call the Friends of Fenwick Island Lighthouse at (301) 250–1098.

The Fenwick Island Light stands just north of the Mason-Dixon Line.

HOOPER STRAIT LIGHT

Saint Michaels, Maryland - 1867

For more than forty years, beginning in 1827, the crooked channel of Hooper Strait was marked by a lightship. But in 1867 the Lighthouse Board built a modest screw-pile tower there to guide shipping. Ten years later, a massive ice floe swept the little lighthouse off its piles and carried it five miles down the bay. A tender found the wreckage and managed to salvage the lens and some of the equipment.

A larger, hexagonal lighthouse had replaced the crushed tower by the autumn of 1879, and it remained in service for three-quarters of a century. Deactivated in 1954, it was eventually acquired by the Chesapeake Bay Maritime Museum in St. Michaels on the Maryland eastern shore. In order to move the forty-four-foot-wide structure down the Chesapeake to St. Michaels, museum officials had it cut in half, like a giant apple, and loaded onto a barge. Reassembled and restored to like-new condition, the lighthouse now stands beside the museum on Navy Point.

After being disassembled and restored, the Hooper Strait Light now stands at the Chesapeake Maritime Museum.

To reach the museum and lighthouse, take US-50 north from Cambridge and then State 33 east to Saint Michaels, a charming Chesapeake Bay community. The museum, which is near the downtown area on Navy Point, is a village in itself, with houses, stores, a restaurant, and wonderful exhibits of small boats used by the bay watermen.

The lighthouse is surrounded by historic workboats and oyster sailboats at nearby docks, giving you the feeling that you have stepped back in time. The Hooper Strait Lighthouse, one of the three remaining screw-pile lighthouses in the Chesapeake Bay, is a cottage-type structure. It was moved to the museum site in 1966 and has been restored and furnished in turn-of-the-century style. If you could only go to one lighthouse, this would be the one to see—even the white-and-red-checkered tablecloth on the kitchen table looks as if the keeper's mug of hot coffee were about to be set upon it.

For more information, contact the Chesapeake Bay Maritime Museum, Box 636, Saint Michaels, Maryland 21663.

Hooper Strait Light, Navy Point

(below) Lighthouse kitchen
(right) Living quarters

Work room at Drum Point Light

Child's bedroom at Drum Point

(top right) Close-up of the light at Drum Point
(bottom right) The Drum Point Light is one of the
few remaining screw-pile lighthouses.

DRUM POINT LIGHT
Solomons, Maryland - 1883

Many screw-pile lighthouses once stood in the shallow Chesapeake, but today, only a few remain. One of these is Drum Point Lighthouse, a hexagonal, cottage-type lighthouse built on ten-inch, wrought-iron piles.

Erected in 1883, the lighthouse cost $5,000 and took only about a month to build. Fitted with a fourth-order Fresnel lens, it showed a fixed red light, warning vessels of the sandy spit off the point. Having served for almost eight decades, Drum Point Light was taken out of active service in 1962.

Take State 4 south from Washington, D.C., to Solomons. The museum and lighthouse are on the left just before the bridge over the Patuxent River. The lighthouse has been wonderfully restored and furnished in early 1900s style. Admission is $1.

The museum is free and offers exhibits on the paleontology, estuarine biology, and maritime history of the region. For hours and additional information, contact Calvert Marine Museum, Box 97, Solomons, Maryland; (301) 326–2042.

CAPE HENRY LIGHT
Virginia Beach, Virginia - 1792

People talked about placing a lighthouse on Cape Henry, at the entrance to the Chesapeake Bay, a long time before anyone actually got around to building one. Among the numerous projects undertaken by Virginia's flamboyant Alexander Spotswood, who governed the colony for the British during the early 1700s, was the construction of a light tower at the mouth of the Chesapeake. Every inch the cavalier, the governor was given to flights of romantic fancy; his ambitious proposals usually generated a great many toasts and a lot of high-toned conversation, but not much action. For instance, in 1716 Spotswood decided to explore the unpopulated wilderness west of the Virginia tidewater, and he actually set off into the backcountry wearing a green velvet riding suit and sporting a sweeping plume in his hat. Spotswood apparently saw his journey into the wilds as something of an extended fox hunt, since he took with him a dozen properly attired Virginia gentlemen and a wagon creaking under a heavy load of wine and liquor. A few days after they had departed, Spotswood and his companions returned to their plantations in much too tipsy a condition to remember anything they had seen.

Spotswood could not interest the British government in his lighthouse idea, but

the governor's proposal attracted numerous advocates in Virginia's House of Burgesses as well as among prominent planters and merchants throughout the Chesapeake region. Like the governor himself, however, they all found it far easier to raise a glass of port than to finance and construct a tall stone tower. Nearly half a century after Spotswood and his plumed hat had passed from the scene, the Cape Henry tower still had not been built.

In 1774 the colonies of Maryland and Virginia finally decided to move ahead with the project. Tons of stone were piled up at the construction site, but funding ran out while the foundation was being laid. Before more money could be found, the drums of the Revolutionary War put a stop to the effort. After the war, stonemasons understandably balked at working for worthless Continental dollars. So, it was not until 1791, shortly after adoption of the Constitution and the establishment of a stable currency, that the project could continue. The nation's first federal Congress authorized a lighthouse for Cape Henry and appropriated $24,077 for its construction.

Contractor John McComb, hired by Secretary of the Treasury Alexander Hamilton, had at first hoped to use the stone stockpiled for the tower by colonial builders twenty years earlier. Unfortunately, most of the big stones had sunk so deep into the sand that they could not be salvaged. Using freshly quarried sandstone, McComb completed the ninety-foot tower in the fall of 1792.

McComb and his crews built a solid lighthouse; the tower has stood for almost 200 years, through several wars and countless gales. The Confederates put the light out of service briefly at the beginning of the Civil War, but the Lighthouse Board had its lamps burning again by 1863.

In 1870 a network of large cracks began to split the tower. Fearing that the lighthouse would crack open and collapse, the board had a cast-iron tower built about 100 yards to the southeast. Standing 156 feet tall, the new tower received a first-order Fresnel lens and began service to the Chesapeake shipping lanes on December 15, 1881. Both towers still stand today.

Both of these lighthouses are located on the grounds of Fort Story at the north end of Virginia Beach. To reach the fort, take US-60 south from Norfolk. The entrance to the fort, an active military post, is about ten miles from downtown Norfolk. The guard at the gate will provide a car pass and directions to the lighthouse.

A National Historic Landmark, the old 1791 lighthouse is open to visitors, who may, if they wish, climb the ninety-foot tower. The companion tower, only a few hundred feet away, however, is still in use and is closed to the public.

For more information, call the Virginia Beach Visitors Information Center at (800) 446-8038.

The pair of lighthouse towers at Cape Henry

FORT MONROE OLD POINT COMFORT LIGHT
Fort Monroe, Virginia - 1802

Among the earliest lighthouses constructed in the Chesapeake Bay itself was a stubby, fifty-four-foot tower built in 1802 at Fort Monroe. The light marked the mouth of the James River and the entrance to Hampton Roads.

Because of its strategic location, the lighthouse saw plenty of conflict; several crucial battles were fought within sight of keepers in the lantern. During the War of 1812, British troops under Admiral Cockburn successfully stormed Fort Monroe and later used the lighthouse as a watchtower. Half a century later, the ironclad *Virginia* steamed past the Point Comfort Light on its way to do battle with the *Monitor*. Following the Civil War, Confederate President Jefferson Davis was imprisoned in a Fort Monroe cell not far from the tower.

Fort Monroe remains an active military post and is the home of the Army Training Command. The lighthouse stands in the middle of Officer's Row.

To reach the fort, drive west from Norfolk on I-64; then take the first exit after you emerge from the tunnel under Hampton Road. The sentry at the Fort Monroe gate can provide directions to the lighthouse.

The tower is not open to the public, but visitors are more than welcome at the Casement Museum, located a short distance from the lighthouse. A self-guided tour starting at the museum leads visitors through the historic fort.

Entrance to the fort and museum are free, and both are open daily from 10:30 A.M. to 5:00 P.M. For more information, call (804) 727–3973.

British troops used the Fort Monroe lighthouse as a watchtower during the War of 1812.

CAPE CHARLES LIGHT

Chesapeake Bay, Virginia - 1828

Some thirty-five years after the Cape Henry Lighthouse began to guide ships into the Chesapeake, a second, smaller tower was built on the opposite lip of the bay. Completed in 1828 at a cost of just under $7,400, the fifty-five-foot Cape Charles Lighthouse did little to improve navigation. Almost from the moment its lamps were lit, skippers complained that the light was hopelessly inadequate. Even under ideal conditions, the light carried only twelve miles, and in heavy weather or fog it could barely be seen at all. Even so, it remained in service for more than three decades before the Lighthouse Board thought of replacing it.

Even the Coast Guard has trouble getting to this lighthouse. Located on a remote island near the northern lip of the Chesapeake Bay, it is not open to the public.

In 1858 the board launched construction of a 150-foot brick tower about a mile from the original Cape Charles Light. But hampered by storms and shortages of materials, the work moved slowly. At the outbreak of the Civil War, three years after the first brick was laid, the tower had reached only half its intended height. In 1862 a party of Confederate raiders attacked the construction site, driving off the work crew and destroying whatever they could. Another two years were needed to repair the damage and complete the tower. The lamps, which illuminated a first-order Fresnel lens, were finally lit on May 17, 1864.

As with many of the other Southern lights, the nemesis of the Cape Charles Lighthouse has been erosion. In 1883 officials measured the rate of erosion on Cape Charles and discovered with alarm that the

The Cape Charles Light's strong-but-lightweight design is unusual for a lighthouse as far north as Virginia.

sea was moving thirty feet closer to the lighthouse each year. Workers tried but failed to stop the advance with stone jetties. Then, an engineering study revealed that halting the erosion would cost $150,000, a truly astounding sum at that time. So the board saw no alternative but to build another tower further from the encroaching waves.

The new Cape Charles Lighthouse was begun in 1892 and completed two years later on a site roughly a mile inland from the original light station. The 191-foot tower is an iron cylinder only nine feet wide, but it is reinforced by a pyramidal steel superstructure. The lantern is reached by means of a staircase inside the cylinder. Because of its design, unusual for a lighthouse as far north as Virginia, the tower is strong but relatively light in weight. Since the members of the superstructure offer little resistance to wind, lighthouses of similar design are often seen along the hurricane-plagued coasts of Florida and the Gulf of Mexico. Now automated, the Cape Charles Light remains in use.

ASSATEAGUE ISLAND LIGHT
Assateague Island, Virginia - 1833

In 1831 Congress appropriated money for a lighthouse to be built a few miles south of the Maryland border on Assateague Island, about halfway between the Chesapeake and Delaware bays. Its chief duty was to warn ships away from the dangerous shoals that extend from the Maryland and Virginia coasts like knife blades; however, after the light was completed and its lamps lit in January 1833, it proved too weak to perform this task effectively. But nothing was done about the problem for almost a quarter century.

Then, during the late 1850s, the Lighthouse Board launched a determined campaign aimed at repairing, upgrading, and correcting the many deficiencies of lighthouses all along the Southern coasts. As part of this comprehensive effort, the board decided to rebuild the Assateague Island tower. The Civil War interrupted the work, and the new lighthouse was not ready for service until October 1867. Once its lamps were lit, however, sailors could easily see the improvement. A first-order Fresnel lens made the light visible from nineteen miles at sea.

The Assateague Island Light is now automated but still active. It stands inside the Chincoteague National Wildlife Refuge, not far from the Assateague Island National Seashore.

To reach the Wildlife Refuge from US-13 (the main road down the eastern shore of Virginia), take State 175 to Chincoteague; then follow signs to the refuge across the bridge to Assateague Island. Depending on the season, there may be a small admission fee to enter the wildlife area, which allows hunting.

Although you can see the lighthouse as you cross the bridge to the island, the tower gets lost behind the trees when you reach land. The person at the tollbooth can provide directions to the tower. A mile or so beyond the tollbooth is a large parking lot on the right side of the paved road. From the parking lot, a trail leads several hundred yards through the woods to the lighthouse.

The tower is painted with red and white stripes and looks something like a candy cane without the curving top. A surf boat and a first-order lens are on display outside at the base of the tower. The tower itself is closed to the public because the lighthouse is still in service.

Try going to the lighthouse in the late afternoon, and if there are not too many other people in the area, you might see wild deer grazing about the tower as darkness falls.

The Assateague Island Light has been active since 1833.

PORTSMOUTH LIGHTSHIP
Portsmouth, Virginia -1916

The job of lighthouses is to guide ships. Ironically, some lighthouses are actually ships themselves. Equipped with lanterns and lenses, these *lightships* are anchored over remote shoals where lighthouses would be too dangerous or too expensive to build.

In 1915 fifty-five lightships were stationed in U.S. waters. But lighthouse builders have since found ways to replace many lightships with permanent off-shore structures, and improvements in navigational aids have made others unnecessary. All but a handful of the old lightships are now gone, and no lightship stations remain.

The vessel now called the Portsmouth Lightship was commissioned in 1916. Known to lighthouse officials as LV 101, it served more than forty-eight years on posts off the coasts of Virginia, Delaware, and Massachusetts. Retired from active service in 1964, the ship was moved to dry land beside the busy waterfront at Portsmouth, Virginia.

The crew's quarters, the galley, and the engine room look as if the crew is just on leave and could return at any moment to take the ship to sea. The beds are made, and the galley appears well stocked for the next meal. Photos and artifacts tell the story of life on a lightship during the early twentieth century.

The lightship, located beside the busy Portsmouth waterfront, is open Tuesday through Saturday from 10:00 a.m. to 5:00 p.m. and Sunday from 2:00 to 5:00 p.m. For more information, call (804) 393–8741.

The Portsmouth Lightship beacon guided sailors off the coasts of Virginia, Delaware and Maryland.

CHAPTER TWO

LIGHTS OF
THE BIG SAND ISLANDS

North Carolina, South Carolina, and Georgia

Lights of The Big Sand Islands

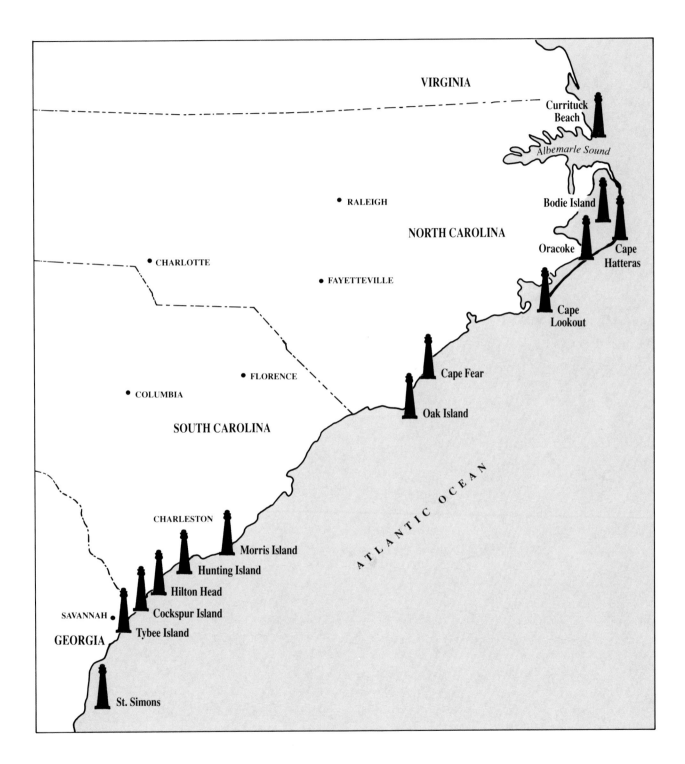

On the last Saturday in June, in the year 1759, a handsome merchant brig known as the *Tyrrel* set sail from New York bound for Antigua in the West Indies. Captain Arthur Cochlan kept the *Tyrrel* close-in, just beyond sight of the land, so that he could take advantage of the coast-hugging Labrador Current. Cochlan's brig made good progress, and by the evening of July 1, it approached Cape Hatteras.

Cochlan planned to keep well to seaward rounding the cape so as to avoid Diamond Shoals, the deadly finger of sand that protrudes some eight miles from Hatteras out into the Atlantic. But in the end, the shoals would not be his chief concern, for just after dark, the *Tyrrel* slammed head-on into a squall.

Hearing the wind claw at the *Tyrrel*'s two big masts, Cochlan ordered his crew to close-reef the topsails. But the wind grew stronger, the waves surged higher, and soon, the *Tyrrel* began to take on water. Cochlan decided to make a run through Hatteras Inlet toward the calmer waters of Pamlico Sound. The *Tyrrel* never made it to the inlet. Just as the ship turned toward land, it was hit by an enormously powerful gust of wind. The *Tyrrel* rolled over on its side and started to sink.

Some members of the crew were below decks when the *Tyrrel* capsized. The impact of the gust threw First Mate Thomas Purnell out of his bunk and against the wall of his cabin. Purnell fought his way to the roundhouse door, where he barely managed to avoid being crushed by a huge ladder that had broken away from the quarterdeck. Soon he was in the water, swimming for his life along with most of his shipmates.

Some of the crew remained with the brig and tried to right it by shifting the weight of its two heavy guns. But Purnell saw that the only hope lay in the lifeboat now floating bottom-side up some distance from the hulk of the doomed *Tyrrel*. Purnell and several other sailors swam out to the boat and managed to turn it over.

Filled with water to within three or four inches of its gunwales, the boat was useless. But the cabin boy, being the lightest member of the crew, slipped on board and set to work with a bucket. In about half an hour he had the boat more or less dry, and half-drowned sailors started to clamber aboard. Eventually, seventeen men were crammed into the boat, which was only nineteen feet long.

Tragically, the carpenter had lost all his tools in the wreck. With a decent chisel he might have been able to cut through the sides of the capsized ship and get at its ample stores. As it was, not a single barrel of fresh water and only one small chest of biscuit could be located among the flotsam littering the water near the sinking brig.

The darkness surrounding the men in the boat was total. Captain Cochlan believed he was very near Cape Hatteras, but in 1759, no lighthouse stood on the cape. If there had been a light burning on the cape that evening, the crew of the *Tyrrel* might not have suffered the awful fate that awaited them. But with his compass ruined by seawater and no stars in the sky, the captain had no way to take bearings. He looked in every direction and saw no lights at all on any horizon. So, with a deep sigh, he pointed, and his men began to pull toward what they desperately hoped was dry land and safety.

At dawn on the following day, Cochlan could see that he had pointed in the wrong direction. There was no land in sight. He had taken his boat toward the east, away from Hatteras. Cochlan's crew turned their little vessel back toward land, but later that day, they encountered a westerly wind that made progress impossible. In fact, the winds blew up into a storm that carried them farther and farther out onto the high sea.

On the third day the men gave up most of their clothing so that the cloth could be stitched into a makeshift sail. Using an oar as mast, they raised their sail, and the sluggish forward motion it gave their boat filled them with hope. Guiding on the sun during the day and the North Star at night, Cochlan maintained a dead-reckoning course for Cape Hatteras. But still he could not find land.

On July 11, after more than nine days in the open boat, Cochlan's men began to die. Some, maddened by thirst, had started to drink seawater. The second mate, who had begun to drink great, heaping handfuls of the killing salt water, was the first to go. An hour or so later, he was followed by the carpenter, who had also taken to drinking seawater. The bodies, by necessity, were dumped overboard.

At dawn, on July 12, a sloop was sighted on the horizon, causing an eruption of shouting and waving on board the *Tyrrel* launch. But the sloop vanished as quickly as it had appeared, and the now hopelessly weakened sailors gave themselves up for lost. By the next morning, three more men had died. Another perished later that same day. Four died on July 14 and three on July 15.

That left only Captain Cochlan, First Mate Purnell, the boatswain, and the cabin boy. Purnell believed the cabin boy would be the last left alive, but on the evening of July 15, the lad breathed his last. The three survivors then made an agonizing decision; they would cut pieces of flesh off the boy's dead body and eat them. In the end, however, they were too squeamish to carry out the plan.

Some days later, Purnell found himself alone in the boat. For nearly a week he drifted in a thick fog, keeping himself alive by scraping barnacles off the sides and rudder of the boat with a knife and chewing them. Then, on July 24, the fog cleared, and on the horizon, Purnell spotted a sail. There was a ship—a sloop headed in his direction.

After more than three weeks in an open boat with no fresh water and only barnacles for food, Purnell was pulled aboard a merchant vessel about two days out from Marblehead, Massachusetts. The *Tyrrel* launch had drifted into the Gulf Stream and been pushed far to the north. The captain of the rescuing ship, a man named Castleman, carried the wretched castaway down to his own cabin and fed him some thin soup. A few days later, Purnell's shriveled feet touched land again at Marblehead.

It took Purnell two months to recover from his ordeal, and by then the American colonies were abuzz over his miraculous survival and rescue. The tragic fate of the *Tyrrel*, with the loss of all but one member of its crew, brought

Rough seas off of Cape Hatteras have caused many shipwrecks.

heated demands that a lighthouse be erected on Cape Hatteras. But more than forty years and a revolution would pass before a lighthouse was finally built on the cape to guide mariners and warn them away from Hatteras's treacherous shoals.

The lamps of the Cape Hatteras Light were first lit during the summer of 1803. By that time, only a few other lighthouses stood on the sandy coasts and barrier islands of the states south of the Chesapeake, the most notable of them at Cape Fear in North Carolina, Charleston Harbor in South Carolina, and Tybee Island near Savannah, Georgia.

But the Lighthouse Service, formed by act of Congress in 1789, was well aware of the dangers the Southern coastline represented to mariners. Obviously, the few lights then in existence were woefully inadequate. Southbound ships had to hug those coasts to avoid fighting the strong northward current of the Gulf Stream. This made them vulnerable to shoals and to being driven ashore by storms. To lessen the dangers, the service (later known as the Lighthouse Board) embarked on a construction program which, after many decades, would dot the Southern coasts with tall lighthouses.

BALD HEAD ISLAND (CAPE FEAR) LIGHT
Bald Head Island, North Carolina - 1796

The federal government erected the first lighthouse in North Carolina at Bald Head to guide ships into the Cape Fear River. Built at a total cost of $7,359, it functioned without incident for more than two decades. Then, in 1818, it was replaced by a new lighthouse with a fixed beam shining from atop a 110-foot tower.

When Captain Henry Hunter of the revenue cutter *Taney* visited Bald Head Island in 1834, he found the lighthouse in the care of "an old revolutionary soldier . . . unable to give the light his constant personal attention." Presumably, the old soldier was soon retired or, at least, was given an assistant to help him light the lantern's fifteen lamps each night.

The lighthouse tower itself would eventually stand in need of help. After federal engineers closed one of the Cape Fear channels, the river water flowing past Bald Head speeded up and began to tear apart the shoreline. By 1883 this galloping erosion threatened the foundation of the lighthouse. But a hastily constructed stone jetty corrected the problem just in time to avert disaster. Less than a month after the jetty was finished, a hurricane roared in from the Caribbean. More than 100 vessels were sunk by this storm, but the lighthouse was saved. Although deactivated in 1935, the tower still stands.

Take State 87 or State 211 from US-17 to Southport, a quaint fishing port with lovely old homes and delightful seafood restaurants. Bald Head Island (called Smith Island on older maps) can be reached only by passenger ferry from Southport; the ferry costs $5 per person, round-trip. A restaurant and restrooms are located near the ferry landing, and the lighthouse is only a few hundred yards away.

The lighthouse withstood an 1883 hurricane during which 100 vessels were sunk.

OCRACOKE LIGHT
Ocracoke Island, North Carolina - 1803

For years, during the early eighteenth century, the notorious pirate Edward Teach, also known as Blackbeard, ravaged the sea lanes off the North Carolina Outer Banks. When not plundering helpless merchant ships, Blackbeard used Ocracoke Inlet as a convenient anchorage, and it was here, on November 21, 1718, that a pair of British sloops finally cornered the pirate.

Blackbeard had his opponents outgunned, and with the eight big cannons on his pirate ship, he shot the two small sloops to splinters. Even so, he could not prevent the stubborn British from boarding his vessel. Armed with pistols and rapiers, the British sailors swarmed over the gunwales behind their young commander, Lieutenant Robert Maynard. At first, the pirates had the upper hand, but they were soon exhausted from the effort of swinging their heavy cutlasses. The British, with their lightweight rapiers, moved in for the kill. Among the pirates cut down in the free-for-all was Blackbeard himself, who received numerous pistol wounds as well as a deep gash in his neck before falling dead on the blood-soaked deck of his ship.

The first Ocracoke Lighthouse was built in 1803 on Shell Castle Island inside the Ocracoke Inlet, not far from Blackbeard's former hideout. Destroyed by lightning on August 16, 1818, it was replaced some six years later by a light on the banks of the inlet near Ocracoke Village. This second light, built in 1823, remains among the oldest lighthouses still active on the Southern coast.

In 1861 Confederate raiders destroyed the fourth-order Fresnel lens. A new lens was placed in the tower in 1864, and the Ocracoke Light has functioned continuously ever since. Located about a mile from the channel it guards, the Ocracoke Lighthouse is considered an inlet light rather than a coastal light.

Ocracoke Island can only be reached by ferry. A ferry leaves Cedar Island, north of the Morehead City/Beaufort area, five times each day; the fare is $5 per car; call (919) 225–3551 for reservations. Another ferry operates out of Swan Quarter off US-264, with two round-trips each day; the cost is $10 per car; call (919) 926–1111. A free ferry run by the state and leaving every half hour during the summer links Hatteras Island with Ocracoke Island.

For more information, contact the Cape Hatteras National Seashore, Route 1, Box 675, Manteo, North Carolina 27954; (919) 473–2111.

The Ocracoke Light guards Blackbeard's former haunts.

CAPE HATTERAS LIGHT
Hatteras Island, North Carolina - 1803

America's Mercury and Apollo astronauts were told to watch for the hook of Cape Hatteras when their orbits carried them over the East Coast of the United States. Hatteras is such a prominent feature, it can easily be distinguished, even from hundreds of miles out in space. But earthly mariners have often had a difficult time seeing the cape, especially at night or in foul weather.

Two mighty rivers in the ocean, the cold Labrador Current flowing down from the north and the warm Gulf Stream sweeping up from the Caribbean, pass close by Cape Hatteras. Their strong currents push ships dangerously close to Hatteras and to Diamond Shoals, the shallow bar extending eight miles out into the ocean. As a result, this stormy coast, known to sailors as the "graveyard of the Atlantic," has claimed more than 2,300 ships since the early 1500s.

During colonial times, the British became all too well acquainted with the dangers of Cape Hatteras and her deadly shoals. The ill-fated *Tyrrel* was only one of countless colonial ships that ended their days in the shallows off the coast of North Carolina. But the British Parliament showed little interest in spending money on lighthouses in America, and nothing was done about placing a light on the cape until after the Revolutionary War.

Congress authorized construction of the Hatteras Lighthouse as early as 1794, but no brick was laid until late in 1799. The delay was caused, in part, by a political tiff over the selection of a contractor. The job eventually went to Henry Dearborn, a Congressman who would later serve as Secretary of War (the town of Dearborn, Michigan, is named after him). Dearborn's crews, tortured by swarms of mosquitoes and outbreaks of yellow fever, needed three years to complete the ninety-five-foot tower. The light finally went into service in October 1803.

Surfboat rescue crew, Cape Hatteras

From the beginning, the Hatteras Light had a spotty reputation as a coastal marker. Fitted with eighteen lamps and fourteen-inch reflectors, the light could supposedly be seen from eighteen miles at sea. But ships' captains complained incessantly that they could not see the light, even when nearing the cape. In a report to the Lighthouse Board in 1851, U.S. Navy Lieutenant David Porter called Hatteras "the worst light in the world."

Describing his many journeys around the cape, Porter said: "The first nine trips I made I never saw Hatteras Light at all, though frequently passing in sight of the breakers, and when I did see it, I could not tell it from a steamer's light, except that the steamers' lights are much brighter." In response to Porter's report and to the numerous complaints received about the Hatteras Light, the Lighthouse Board ordered the tower raised to 150 feet and had it fitted with a first-order Fresnel lens.

At the beginning of the Civil War, the Confederates removed the lens and destroyed the lighting apparatus. The Union had the lighthouse back in service again by June 1862, but mariners still considered it inadequate to its task. So, following the war, the board replaced it with a new, 193-foot brick tower, making Hatteras the tallest brick lighthouse in the United States.

The revolving first-order Fresnel lens atop the new tower was in operation by mid-December 1871. Shortly afterward, the old tower was blown up to keep it from falling over in a storm and damaging the new lighthouse or, perhaps, crushing some hapless assistant keeper. After the demolition, the keeper reported sadly that the "old landmark was spread out on the beach, a mass of ruins." The keeper's sentiments aside, sailors agreed that the new lighthouse was a considerable improvement over its predecessor.

The big brick tower, painted with spiral stripes, has stood up to many storms. In 1879 a lightning bolt of extraordinary power opened large cracks in its masonry walls, but the structure remained sound. However, the lighthouse and its keepers soon faced a much more serious threat from beach erosion. By World War I the sea had moved to within 100 yards of the lighthouse. By 1935 high tides brought waves to within a few feet of the foundation. Fearing the water would undercut the structure, officials removed the lens and apparatus, placing them in a skeleton tower erected safely inland. The sea reversed itself, however, and in just a few years' time, replaced much of the beach it had previously gobbled up. By 1950 the Coast Guard thought it safe to reactivate the Hatteras Light. Now automated, the lighthouse is part of the Cape Hatteras National Seashore.

The Hatteras Light can be reached on paved road by taking US-64 at Manteo or US-158 down the Outer Banks past Kitty Hawk to the entrance of the National Seashore. State 12 runs more than forty miles down the barrier dune islands. To reach the lighthouse, turn off State 12 at the village of Buxton. The tower is visible for miles.

Pieces of the Civil War ironclad Monitor and other bits of "the graveyard of the Atlantic" are on display in a small maritime museum operated by the park service. The tower is now closed to the public because of structural weakness. Park-service interpreters give regularly scheduled talks.

For additional information, contact the Cape Hatteras National Seashore, Route 1, Box 675, Manteo, North Carolina 27954; (919) 473-2111.

The Cape Hatteras Light is visible for miles.

CAPE LOOKOUT LIGHT
Cape Lookout National Seashore, North Carolina -1812

The harbor guarded by Cape Lookout has long been a place of refuge for mariners sailing under the flags of many nations as well as under the skull and crossbones of piracy. Blackbeard is said to have dropped anchor in the harbor. It was used as an anchorage by the British during the Revolutionary War and by the U.S. Navy during two world wars. But the headland protecting this safe harbor from the open sea has always been considered extremely dangerous. Very early on, Cape Lookout earned the title *Promontorium Tremendum*, or "Horrible Headland," by smashing the hulls of ships that strayed too close to its hidden shoals.

Congress authorized a lighthouse for Cape Lookout in 1804, not long after the completion of the Hatteras Light. But as with the Hatteras Light and many other Southern lighthouses, there were long delays in construction of the tower, and it was not lighted until 1812. This first Cape Lookout Lighthouse cost $20,678 to build and was of unusual design. It consisted of an inner tower of brick enveloped by an outer cocoon of wood.

Painted with red and white stripes, the tower rose 104 feet above the water, but its light was surprisingly weak. Skippers often had a difficult time seeing it, particularly at night. David Porter, now a mail-steamer captain, complained that on more than one occasion he almost ran up on the shoals while looking for the light.

To improve the light's performance, the Lighthouse Board had a new, 156-foot tower constructed in 1859, fitting it with a first-order Fresnel lens. Confederates retreating from nearby Fort Macon knocked out the lens, but the board quickly replaced it with a third-order Fresnel, and the light remained in service. In 1873 the tower was painted with the unusual diamond pattern that still distinguishes it from other lights today.

To reach the Cape Lookout National Seashore, take US-70 north through Morehead City and Beaufort; at Otway follow the signs to Harkers Island; then follow the paved road to the ferry dock. Twice a day the ferry carries passengers only (no cars) to the barrier island where the lighthouse is located; the ferry leaves Harkers Island at 9:00 A.M. and 1:00 P.M.; the cost is $10 for adults. For reservations, call (919) 728–3866. Be sure to take water, food, and bug spray; there are no facilities on the barrier island.

Maintained by the Coast Guard, the lighthouse is not open to the public. But the trip to the barrier island is still worthwhile—the beaches and island are part of the National Seashore and are kept in their natural state.

For additional information, contact the Cape Lookout National Seashore, Box 690, Beaufort, North Carolina 28516; (919) 728–2121.

(right) The Cape Lookout Light has warned sailors for years of the dangerous, hidden shoals off the headland.

BODIE ISLAND LIGHT
Bodie Island, North Carolina -1847

In 1837 Congress sent Lieutenant Napoleon Coste, commander of the revenue cutter *Campbell,* to inspect the dark coasts south of the Chesapeake. After rounding Cape Henry and losing sight of its sandstone lighthouse tower, Coste found no other worthwhile navigational markers until he reached Cape Hatteras, more than 150 miles to the south. Coste reported that a lighthouse was urgently needed to fill in this huge blind spot. He recommended that the new lighthouse be located on Bodie Island, at the northern end of the Outer Banks, where "more vessels are lost . . . than on any other part of our coast."

With Coste's report in hand, Congress appropriated $5,000 to build a lighthouse on Bodie, but squabbles over the location and the design of the tower caused a ten-year delay in construction. Workmen did not start laying brick until late in the summer of 1847.

The contractor on the project was Francis Gibbons, of Baltimore, who would later become prominent as a builder of lighthouses on the rugged West Coast. Unfortunately, the highly competent Gibbons was not allowed to design the tower. Instead, he was handed a plan for a squat, ungainly structure only fifty-four feet high and measuring seventeen feet in diameter at the base and twelve feet in diameter at the top.

Gibbons was forced to work under the thumb of an ex-customs inspector who knew little about construction and even less about lighthouse towers. Although Gibbons and his men struck mud only a few feet below the Bodie Island sands, the contractor was told to drive no piles. Instead, he was instructed to lay down a shallow foundation of brick. As a result, the tower was highly unstable, and soon after it was completed in 1848, it began to lean sickeningly toward the sea.

Within two years of construction, the tower was already a foot out of plumb and leaning further to the east with each passing day. To keep the lighthouse from toppling over, the government spent $1,400 trying to straighten it. But the tower continued to wobble on its unsteady base, leaning first one way and then another.

Bodie Island Lighthouse by moonlight

38

By 1859, the Bodie Island Lighthouse had deteriorated beyond the possibility of repair, and the Lighthouse Board secured a $25,000 appropriation from Congress to erect a new tower. Built on sturdy piles, the new lighthouse was eighty feet tall. Its lantern held a third-order Fresnel lens, but its lamps, first lit on July 1, 1859, would burn for little more than two years. In the fall of 1861 Confederate troops stacked explosives inside the tower and blew it apart.

A third Bodie Island Lighthouse was completed in 1871 with materials left over from construction of a new tower at Cape Hatteras. Rising 156 feet above sea level, the Bodie tower held aloft a first-order Fresnel lens that made its light visible from nineteen miles at sea. Within a month of the lighting, a flock of geese crashed into the lantern, badly damaging the lens, but it was repaired and is still in use today. The Bodie tower is painted with white and black horizontal bands for better visibility as a daymark.

The lighthouse is located on State 12 a few miles south of the National Seashore entrance. A sign points the way to the tower, which is located on a paved road less than a mile off State 12. The park service operates a visitors center in the old keeper's house. Since Bodie is still a working lighthouse, it is closed to the public, but its classic tower is well worth a stop.

For additional information, contact the Cape Hatteras National Seashore, Route 1, Box 675, Manteo, North Carolina 27954; (919) 473-2111.

The lighthouse at dusk

CURRITUCK BEACH LIGHT
Corolla, North Carolina - 1874

Its lamps first lit in 1874, the Currituck Beach Lighthouse illuminated one of the last remaining dark stretches of Southern coastline. Strategically placed about halfway between the Cape Henry, Virginia, and Bodie Island lights, the Currituck Lighthouse serves a forty-mile stretch of coast where southbound ships often come perilously close to the shore. Captains keep their ships close-in when heading south in order to avoid the strong northward current of the Gulf Stream.

Because the Currituck tower was built on sand, it was given a strong foundation of heavy timber cribbing. The foundation has remained solid for more than 100 years under the weight of the brick tower, which stands 158 feet above sea level on Whale's Head Hill at Currituck Beach. The light is visible from nineteen miles at sea.

Take US-158 to the north side of Kitty Hawk. Where US-158 turns west, take the unnumbered road to Corolla. The unpainted tower is located on the same side of the road as Currituck Sound. Neither the lighthouse nor the keeper's dwelling are open to the public.

The high-powered light at Currituck Beach is visible from nineteen miles at sea.

OAK ISLAND LIGHT
Caswell Beach, North Carolina - 1958

Built in the late 1950s, the Oak Island Lighthouse is among the most recent and innovative of Southern lighthouse towers. Constructed of reinforced concrete, the 169-foot tower looks much like a farm silo. Its builders used a moving slip-form construction technique developed in Sweden. Concrete poured into the form was allowed to dry, and then the form was moved up so that a new section could be poured. The tower never needs painting since its colors were mixed into the wet concrete. The lantern frame and floor are of lightweight aluminum. Using a powerful airport beacon, the Oak Island Light marks the entrance of North Carolina's historic Cape Fear River.

More than a century before construction of today's Oak Island tower, the Treasury Department built a pair of lighthouses on the island to mark the channel over the river bar. When sailors saw one light directly above the other, they knew they were in mid-channel. The more elevated of the two lights was mounted on a tram railway so that it could be moved whenever the channel shifted.

If approaching from south of Wilmington, take State 211 east from Supply to State 133. If driving from Wilmington, take State 87 south to State 133. When State 133 ends, continue for several miles along an unnumbered paved road. The lighthouse is not open to the public.

The 169-foot Oak Island Lighthouse is made of reinforced concrete.

CHARLESTON LIGHT
Morris Island, South Carolina - 1767

A copper plate inserted in the cornerstone of the Charleston Lighthouse reads, "The First Stone of this beacon was laid on the 30th of May 1767 in the seventh year of his Majesty's Reign, George the III." Built by the British colony of South Carolina a few years after the conclusion of the French and Indian War, the Charleston Lighthouse was for decades the only significant navigational light on the southern coasts of America. Located on Morris Island at the entrance to Charleston Harbor, the lighthouse guided ships first with beacons of burning pitch and oakum, then large tallow candles, and later spider lamps.

With the passage of the Lighthouse Act, among the first measures enacted by Congress under the Constitution, the federal government inherited the Charleston Lighthouse. In 1800 Congress spent $5,000—a princely sum in that day—repairing and fitting it with an updated lighting apparatus. But by 1837 the old lighthouse had been replaced by a tower built on what was then called Lighthouse Island. The new tower, not far from Fort Sumter, stood 102 feet from base to lantern and had a revolving light. It received a first-order Fresnel lens in 1858, less than three years before the outbreak of the Civil War.

In April of 1861, with war on the horizon, the governor of secessionist South Carolina demanded that the federal government surrender the lighthouse along with all other markers and buoys in the harbor. The Lighthouse Board inspector stationed at Charleston told his superiors in Washington that the governor had, in no uncertain terms, "requested" him to leave the state.

The board gave up the Charleston Light without a fight, but President Lincoln refused to order his troops to abandon nearby Fort Sumter. As a result, the first battle of the fratricidal "War Between the States" was fought practically in the shadow of the Charleston Lighthouse. The Confederates of South Carolina won the battle, forcing Union troops at Fort Sumter to strike their colors.

The Confederates held Charleston for most of the war, but they could not control the seas beyond the city's once busy harbor. The U.S. Navy imposed a tight blockade, and not long after the fall of Sumter, a Union fleet fol-lowed the lighthouse bea-

con into the Charleston Harbor in an effort to take the city by sea. The attacking fleet was driven off by artillery at Fort Wagner and Fort Gregg, both located on Lighthouse Island. Soon after the attack, the Confederates darkened the light.

Although the naval assault on Charleston failed, the blockade of Southern coasts soon began to strangle the Confederacy. Increasingly desperate, the Southerners made a variety of innovative attempts to break the blockade. One of the most dramatic of these efforts took place within sight of the Charleston Lighthouse tower when, on February 17, 1864, the Confederates staged the world's first successful torpedo attack with a submarine. That night, a thirty-five-foot submersible with six men on board sailed out of Charleston Harbor to take on the Union fleet.

Designed by a now-forgotten inventor, the little submarine had earned a reputation among Southern sailors as more of a coffin than a warship. In testing, it had sunk to the bottom of the harbor repeatedly, dragging several brave volunteer crews to their deaths. During one such test, the designer himself was drowned. Now the unlucky submarine was to be tried in battle.

Unseen by watchful gunners on the Northern ships, the Confederate submarine closed in on its prey, the Union warship *Housatonic*. Gliding along just below the surface, the submarine pushed a torpedo, tied to the end of a long pole, into the side of the federal ship. The torpedo exploded, blowing a gaping hole in the hull of the *Housatonic*, which sank in a matter of minutes. Apparently, the submarine was blown apart by the explosion. Neither the tiny submersible nor its crew were ever seen again.

When federal forces finally captured Charleston by land invasion in 1865, they discovered that the Charleston Lighthouse tower had been destroyed. The Lighthouse Board soon learned that the neglected harbor itself had also suffered damage in the war; old channels had been silted over and new ones had been opened up by the tides. To guide ships effectively through the radically altered channels, a new light was needed. After some years of indecision the board let a contract for a lighthouse to be built on the site of the old colonial tower.

Begun in 1874, the new tower took two years to build. Workmen drove piles fifty feet into the mud beneath the island, pouring onto them an eight-foot-thick concrete foundation, and on this solid base, they raised a brick tower 161 feet high. The lighthouse, placed in service on October 1, 1876, was indeed well built. It survived a major hurricane in 1885 and the following year, an earthquake, which devastated much of Charleston.

Sometime prior to 1892, the tower was painted black with white bands to make it easier to use as a daymark. Charleston Light on Morris Island was replaced in 1962 by a new lighthouse on Sullivan's Island. The Coast Guard planned to tear down the old tower, but a local citizens group, led by the son of a former Charleston Lighthouse keeper, successfully fought to preserve the structure.

Take US-17 south from Charleston. After crossing the Ashley River, turn left onto State 171 and follow it to Folley Beach. About a block before State 171 ends at the Atlantic Ocean, turn left onto East Ashley Street and follow it for several miles until it ends at the gate to the U.S. Coast Guard station. Leave your car in the parking area about 100 yards from the gate and follow the path over the dunes to the beach. The lighthouse stands about a quarter mile north on a sandbar separated from the island by erosion.

HUNTING ISLAND LIGHT
Hunting Island State Park, South Carolina - 1859

The Lighthouse Board had a tower constructed on Hunting Island, about halfway between Charleston and Savannah, in 1859. During the Civil War, the Hunting Island Light went dark along with most of the other Southern lights, and by the end of the war the tower had mysteriously disappeared. No one knows for sure whether the tower was destroyed by the Confederates or was so badly undermined by erosion that it fell into the sea.

In 1875 another tower was built within a mile of the original light station. Constructed of interchangeable cast-iron sections that could be dismantled and reassembled when necessary, the ninety-five-foot tower was lined with bricks. A three-story keeper's house, an oil house, and several outbuildings stood near the tower.

All of these structures were soon threatened by the sea. Gnawing continuously at the land, the waves moved to within 150 feet of the tower and only 60 feet from the keeper's dwelling by 1887. When a series of jetties and revetments failed to stop the advancing water, the board decided to move the station. In 1889 the cast-iron tower was dismantled and rebuilt more than a mile inland.

The light, which is no longer in service, had a second-order Fresnel lens and could be seen from eighteen miles away. The top of the tower is 140 feet from the ground and is reached by a staircase of 181 steps.

To reach this lighthouse, take US-21 east from Beaufort to Hunting Island State Park. A beautiful coastal woodland, the park is well worth the $2 admission. A paved road, curving under the trees, leads to the lighthouse, where you can climb the old iron stairs to the top. Several of the original lighthouse outbuildings—probably used for storing oil and other supplies—are still intact.

The original Hunting Island Light mysteriously disappeared by the end of the Civil War. Confederate destruction or natural erosion?

HARBOUR TOWN LIGHT
(OR HILTON HEAD LIGHT)
Hilton Head Island, South Carolina - 1970

This lighthouse, built in 1970 at Harbour Town on Hilton Head Island, South Carolina, was the first tower to be privately financed since 1817. The ninety-foot-high, red-and-white-striped structure provides a popular symbol for the Sea Pines Plantation development.

Situated on the mainland side of the island, the light serves the Inland Waterway and Calibogue Sound. It flashes a white light every 2.5 seconds. An earlier lighthouse built on Hilton Head Island in 1881 still stands, but it is no longer in use. Its lantern, 136 feet above sea level, was reached by means of a grueling climb up a 112-step staircase.

When a giant hurricane hit the island in 1898, keeper Adam Fripp, a widower, hurried up the steps of the lighthouse to tend the lamps. Close at his heels was his twenty-year-old-daughter, Caroline, who wore a long blue dress. At the height of the storm, an explosive gust of wind blew out the glass in the lantern, extinguishing the lamps. At this critical moment, the keeper was struck by a fatal heart attack.

Although dying, Fripp urged his daughter to relight the lamps. He admonished her to keep them burning, and this she did all through the night of the storm and several nights thereafter. But Caroline never recovered from the strain of those long, lonely nights nor from the grief she suffered over the death of her father. She died about three weeks later.

Over the years, residents and visitors to Hilton Head Island have reported occasional sightings of a ghostly female figure in a blue dress. There have also been reports of mysterious wails and sobbing heard in the vicinity of the now-abandoned lighthouse and of the keeper's dwellings, now moved to Harbour Town.

The lighthouse stands at the entrance to the harbor, which is part of Sea Pines Plantation. Take US-278 until it ends on the island at Sea Pines Plantation. Admission to the grounds is $3. The lighthouse is open to the public every day from 8:00 A.M. to dusk, and visitors can climb to the top for an excellent view of the harbor. They are also welcome to tour the keeper's houses, which were moved from the old lighthouse.

A much older lighthouse, built near Palmetto Dunes in 1890, is still standing but is no longer in operation. Located on private property, this tower is not open to the public.

TYBEE ISLAND LIGHT
Tybee Island, Georgia - 1791

Located at the mouth of the Savannah River in Georgia, the Tybee Island Light was among the first of the South's great lighthouses. General James Oglethorpe commissioned a navigational marker for the commercially strategic river mouth soon after he established the colony of Georgia in 1733. On orders from Oglethorpe, William Blytheman built a ninety-foot, octagonal tower of wood on Tybee Island in 1736. The wood-frame tower could not stand up to the power of ocean gales, and a year or so after it was built, a storm knocked it down.

The smashed marker was replaced in 1742 by a second wooden tower, this one ninety-four feet tall and topped by a thirty-foot flagpole. Eventually, this tower also fell to the wind and sea, as did yet another built in 1757 and a fourth, constructed in 1773. Intended only as daymarks, none of the early Tybee towers displayed a light.

The federal government took possession of the Tybee marker in 1791 and for the first time fitted it with a lamp. The keeper used candles for the light, as was the practice in most lighthouses at that time. Flame and wood, however, are a dangerous combination; and only about a year after Tybee began to display its light, the wooden structure was destroyed by fire. Savannah customs inspector Jesse Tay happened to be on hand when the fire broke out, and he later described the disaster in the following quaint language: "i jumped up and run up Stairs . . . the glass and sinders was fawling so thick and it was so very hot i was not able to tarry half a moment and i saw it was in vain to attempt to save it."

Rebuilt, this time with brick instead of wood, the tower was fitted with Winslow Lewis's lamps and reflectors. The Lewis system employed a smokeless, hollow-wicked oil lamp of a type invented by Ami Argond in 1781. The Argond lamp allowed air to flow freely around and through the wick, thus producing a bright light equal to that of seven candles. Lewis placed the lamp at the center of a large parabolic reflector, which intensified and focused the light. In 1822 a second, shorter tower was built some distance from the main lighthouse. Pilots who saw the two lights vertically aligned one atop the other knew their ships were in mid-channel. In 1857 the main tower was raised to 100 feet and fitted with a second-order Fresnel lens.

The renovated lighthouse had been in use for only about five years when the Union Army invaded Tybee Island and used it as a staging area for attacks on the Confederates at nearby Fort Pulaski. As they retreated, the Confederates exploded a keg of gunpowder in the tower, setting the lighthouse on fire and putting it out of service for the duration of the Civil War.

Federal troops attempted to restore the fire-gutted tower, but an outbreak of cholera hampered the effort. Work ceased altogether when the foreman and four workers died of the disease. As a result, the restoration was not finished until nearly two years after the war. When the work was at last complete and the lamps relit on October 1, 1867, the brick Tybee Island tower reached 144 feet above sea level. Fitted with a first-order Fresnel lens, it projected a beam visible from almost twenty miles at sea.

In 1871 and again in 1878, Tybee was hit with storms so powerful that they cracked the tower. Then, in 1886, an earthquake lengthened the cracks and broke the lens. A Lighthouse Board inspector noted: "The earthquake of last August extended the cracks that have been observed in this tower for several years and made some new ones. . . . The lens was displaced and the attachments to its upper ring were broken."

The board concluded that the tower must be rebuilt, but Congress refused to provide the funds. Consequently, the old tower still stands today, looking much as it did just after the Civil War. Once painted black with a thirty-foot white ring around its midsection, the Tybee Lighthouse is now painted white for the first third of its height, with the remainder painted dark gray.

The Tybee Museum exhibits artifacts and other memorabilia of Tybee from the seventeenth century through World War II. A submarine periscope allows visitors to view the beach and lighthouse from inside the museum.

Take US-80 east from Savannah to Tybee Island. The lighthouse, which can be seen from several miles away, is at the north end of the island in old Fort Screven. The tower can be climbed for breathtaking views of the Atlantic, the Savannah River, the ruins of Fort Screven, and the Victorian homes on Officer's Row. There is a museum at the fort. Admission is $1 each for the lighthouse and museum. The lighthouse is open from 1:00 to 5:00 P.M. daily during the summer and from 1:00 to 5:00 P.M. Thursday through Monday during the winter. Call (912) 786–4077 for more information.

During the Civil War, the Union Army used the island to stage attacks on Confederates at nearby Fort Pulaski. In retaliation the Confederates set the lighthouse on fire.

ST. SIMONS LIGHT
St. Simons Light, Georgia - ca. 1810

Lighthouse keepers and their assistants were not always the closest of friends. One Sunday morning in March 1880, the St. Simons lighthouse keeper, Fred Osborn, fought a duel with his assistant keeper on the front lawn of the lighthouse. The assistant got the better of the fight and shot Osborn dead.

In 1907 Carl Svendsen, his wife, and their dog, Jinx, moved to the then-almost deserted island to tend the light. The Svendsens happily went about their professional and domestic business, unaware of the murder that had taken place there twenty-seven years earlier. Mrs. Svendsen always waited for her husband to clamber down the tower stairs from the light room before she laid dinner on the table. One evening, hearing a heavy tread on the steps, she put out the food as usual. But this time, when the shoes reached the bottom step, her husband did not appear. Jinx barked an alarm and then scampered for safety.

Mrs. Svendsen climbed the lighthouse steps to look for her husband and found him still at the top of the tower. She told him what she had heard, and at first, Svendsen feared his wife had gone daft in the isolation of their lighthouse station. Then, a few days later, he himself heard the phantom footsteps.

The Svendsens lived in the tower for forty years without ever finding an explanation for the bodiless footsteps that never failed to send Jinx into a frenzy. Although the tower is no longer operating, the footsteps are still heard by visitors. Most who hear them believe they are the steps of Fred Osborn.

The original lighthouse was built in 1810 at the southern extremity of St. Simons Island east of Brunswick, Georgia, to mark the St. Simons Sound. Constructed of brick, the tower was a white, tapered octagonal structure seventy-five feet tall. It was topped by a ten-foot iron lantern lit by oil lamps held in suspension by chains. Serving first as a harbor light, it was raised to the status of a coastal light in 1857 when the Lighthouse Board installed a third-order Fresnel lens.

The tower and all the light-station outbuildings were destroyed by Confederate troops in 1862 as they retreated from the island. Following the war, the board let a contract to build a new station with a 100-foot tower. As was the case with the building of many Southern lighthouses, a mysterious sickness—probably yellow fever—plagued the construction crew. The contractor himself fell ill and died in 1870. One of the bondsmen took charge of construction in order to protect his investment, but he, too, fell victim to illness shortly after his arrival. The tower was completed by a second bondsman, and the lamps were lit on September 1, 1872. The new tower, painted white, had a focal plane 104 feet above sea level.

Take the St. Simons Island causeway east from Brunswick; once on the island, take Kings Way to the south end of the island. The lighthouse is located at the end of Kings Way, with a shopping area and post office nearby. The white tapering tower and the classic keeper's house are some of the best examples of American lighthouse architecture in the South.

There is a small parking area close to the front door of the keeper's quarters, which houses the Museum of Coastal History. The $1.50 admission fee is good for both the museum and the lighthouse. The climb to the top of the 106-foot-tall tower provides a grand view of the island.

The lighthouse and museum are open daily except Mondays and some holidays. Call (912) 638–4666 for more information.

The St. Simons Light has an interesting past. A murder was committed there in 1880, and visitors claim that the victim haunts the lighthouse station.

COCKSPUR ISLAND LIGHT
Cockspur Island, Georgia - ca. 1848

The Cockspur Island Light, also known as the South Channel Light, was lit in 1848 along with its companion, the North Channel Light. The two lights guided ships up the Savannah River past Tybee Island, around Elba and Cockspur islands, into Savannah, Georgia.

Like most lights along the Southern coasts, these two lighthouses were darkened by the Civil War. The North Channel Light, built on Oyster Bed Island, did not survive the fighting. But the South Channel Light, located at the eastern end of Cockspur Island, proved luckier. Although it stood in the direct line of fire during the terrific artillery duel between Confederate batteries at Fort Pulaski and the big Union guns on Tybee Island, the South Channel Light escaped the battle without a scratch.

The Cockspur Island Light was relit following the war and continued in service until 1949, when it was permanently retired. After several years of neglect, the

lighthouse was deeded to the National Park Service. Restored in 1978, it is now open to the public.

A poignant story is told about Florence Martus, the sister of George W. Martus, who served for many years as keeper of Cockspur Island Light. For most of her life, Florence lived with her brother in a cottage on nearby Elba Island. One fine day in 1887, several sailors, whose ship had docked at Savannah, rowed across to Fort Pulaski, where Florence was spending the afternoon with her father. Florence's father, who had fought at Pulaski, offered to give the sailors a tour of the island. While her father reminisced about his Civil War days, Florence caught the eye of one of the seamen.

A handsome young man, the sailor asked if he could call on her. She agreed. He visited Florence three times while his ship was in port, and before he left, he promised to return and marry her.

"I'll wait for you always," she told him. As his ship sailed with the high tide on the morning following their last meeting, Florence stood in front of her cottage and waved a white handkerchief. No one knows if the sailor waved back at her.

Florence's sailor never returned, and for more than fifty years she continued to wave in vain at every passing ship. But having lost the love of a particular seaman, she won the hearts of mariners in general. Every year more and more sailors watched for her handkerchief as they passed her cottage. Often they brought her gifts from distant ports they had visited. One sailor even brought her a llama from Peru.

Take US-80 east from Savannah. The tower can be seen from the US-80 bridge. The lighthouse stands on an oyster bed off Tybee Island, and the adventuresome can reach it by wading or swimming, depending on the tide. The Park Service, however, recommends renting a boat.

CHAPTER THREE

LIGHTS OF
THE TREASURE SHOALS

Florida Peninsula

Spanish ships are wrecked, with more than 1,000 crewmen and passengers drowned. Perhaps another 1,500 people survive the disaster by swimming ashore or by hanging onto floating pieces of debris and planking torn off their ships by the storm.

HAVANA HARBOR, JULY 13, 1733

At daybreak, a convoy of twenty-two treasure ships called the Nueva España Flota sets sail for Spain. Two days later the convoy runs head-on into hurricane-force winds blowing out of the north. The Flota commander, Don Rodrigo de Torres, orders his captains to hurry back to Cuba. But soon the winds swing around to the south, cutting the ships off from the safety of Havana Harbor and driving them into the Florida Keys. By nightfall, all twenty-two ships are wrecked. The total number of lives lost is not known. The total value of the treasure lost is also not known, but one of the wrecked ships, the *Capitana El Rubi*, sunk off Key Largo, carried more than five million pesos in silver and gold. Another, the *Almarita El Gallo*, carried precious metals valued at more than four million pesos.

GULF OF FLORIDA, OCTOBER 22, 1752

A hurricane wrecks more than a dozen merchant ships. Lost are the British merchantmen *Alexander, Lancaster, Dolphin, Queen Anne*, and *May*, the colonial merchantmen *Rhode Island* and *Statea*, an unidentified Spanish man-of-war, and several other unidentified Spanish sailing ships.

GULF OF FLORIDA, JUNE 5, 1816

A series of powerful gales wreck several U.S. merchant vessels off Cape Florida and in the keys. Lost are the *Atlas*, the *Martha Brae*, the *Cossack*, the *General Pike*, and the *Zanga*.

SANDY KNIFE IN THE SEA

By the nineteenth century, the Florida peninsula, together with the chain of low, sandy islands (known as keys) extending westward from its southern tip, was well established as the world's most formidable navigational obstacle. Countless ships and untold thousands of lives had been lost to its shoals and unmarked headlands. Although entire Spanish fleets were wiped out in storm-driven collisions with the Florida coast, there is no clear evidence that the Spanish ever erected any lighthouses there.

But the United States, which took possession of Florida in 1821, could not afford to be as lax as the Spanish had been in the matter of lighthouse construction. Following the Louisiana Purchase in 1803, the seas around Florida had become the young nation's busiest highway for commerce. Since the great wall of the Appalachian Mountains divided the rich farm and cattle lands of the Mississippi Basin from the populous cities of the East Coast, western produce had to be shipped to market by sea. Timber, grain, and livestock were floated down the big muddy western rivers in flatboats to New Orleans and other ports and then loaded onto sailing vessels for the journey eastward to the U.S. Atlantic coast or to Europe.

The voyage invariably took merchant ships around the southern tip of Florida, and every year the treacherous Florida coasts exacted a heavy toll of ships, crews, and cargoes. Wrecks occurred with such regularity that salvaging lost cargo grew into a major industry. A thriving town, almost entirely supported by the salvaging business, took root on Key West. There, dozens of salvaging crews, called "wreckers," worked year-round pulling bales of cotton, loads of lumber, and other valuable goods from the smashed hulls of ships that had run aground off Florida.

Clearly, something had to be done to warn ships away from Florida's dangerous shoals and headlands. The effort of marking the Florida Keys began in 1825, when a sixty-five-foot brick lighthouse was erected at Key West. By the following year, similar lighthouses stood on Garden Key, Sand Key, Cape Florida, and the Dry Tortugas, located about seventy miles west of Key West. In the decades that followed, lights also appeared at the mouth of the St. Johns River, Amelia Island, Cape Canaveral, and Jupiter Inlet. The Lighthouse Board hoped to define Florida "from end to end by a band of light." Although the board never achieved this ambitious goal, the new lighthouses made navigation safer and significantly reduced the number of wrecks.

Ironically, the Florida lighthouses were themselves only a little safer than the ships they guided along the coast. Even more exposed than their cousins to the north, these lighthouses were regularly battered by wind, rain, and high water. They lay under constant threat of gale and hurricane. A newly constructed brick tower erected just south of Daytona Beach in 1835 was overwhelmed so quickly that it never got a chance to display its light. Oil for the lamps had still not been delivered when a powerful storm undermined its foundation, and the tower toppled over.

The sea and the wind were not the only dangers. War darkened the Florida coast on more than one occasion. One Florida lighthouse was even attacked by Indians.

BURNED BY INDIANS

By the mid-1830s the Seminoles had had their fill of the white man's broken promises, and war swept like a hurricane over the Florida peninsula. The isolated white settlements, which had sprung up since the arrival of the Americans in Florida, were open to attack. Especially vulnerable were the new lighthouses and their keepers.

On the afternoon of July 23, 1836, keeper John Thompson stepped from the dwelling-house kitchen of the Cape Florida Lighthouse on Biscayne Bay and was astonished to see a large war party of Indians running across a field toward him. Thompson shouted a warning to his assistant, an old black man named Henry, and the two rushed inside the brick-walled lighthouse. They had barely enough time to bar the door before the Indians piled up against it.

Thompson and Henry drove their attackers back with muskets. But the Indians answered with musket fire of their own, peppering the brick walls, splintering the door, and perforating a tin tank containing 225 gallons of lamp oil. Streams of oil squirted through the holes in the tank, soaking the floor and walls as well as the keeper and his helper. Flaming arrows set fire to the door, which in turn, ignited the oil.

The defenders temporarily escaped the conflagration by scrambling up the wooden lighthouse steps. Once at the top, Thompson tried to cut away the steps so the Indians could not follow. But he gave up the effort when he saw that the flames were rapidly climbing after him, consuming the steps as they came. Thompson and Henry took refuge in the lantern, which was constructed mainly of iron, but the metal was already scorching hot. Both men realized, in horror, that they would soon be roasted alive.

"At last the awful moment arrived," Thompson wrote in his account of the attack. "The crackling flames burst around me. The savages at the same time began their hellish yells. My poor Negro looked at me with tears in his eyes, but he could not speak."

Once more Thompson and Henry tried to escape the fire, this time by climbing out onto the narrow, metal platform surrounding the gallery. There they lay flat on their bellies to avoid being shot by the Seminoles, who still had their muskets ready. "The lantern was now full of flame," said Thompson, "the lamps and glasses bursting and flying in all directions."

The iron beneath the men grew so hot that they could no longer bear the pain of touching it. Thompson had brought a musket and a keg of gunpowder with him to the lantern. He now jumped up and threw the powder keg down into the burning lighthouse. He meant to blow up the tower and put himself and his friend out of their misery, taking, he hoped, a few of the hated Seminoles along with him. With a tremendous roar the keg exploded, rocking the tower. But, said Thompson, "it had not the desired effect of blowing me into eternity." Instead, the explosion knocked out the flames.

By this time, Henry was already dead. He had tried to stand and was cut down by an Indian musket ball. And although the fire had died down, Thompson thought of jumping off the tower and joining his friend in death. "I was almost as bad off as before," he said, "a burning fever on me, my feet shot to pieces, no clothes to cover me, nothing to eat or drink, a hot sun overhead, a dead man by my side, no friend near or any to expect, and placed between seventy and eighty feet from the earth with no chance of getting down."

But friends were on the way. Sailors on the U.S. Navy schooner *Concord* had heard the explosion, and the warship soon appeared in the bay within sight of the ruined, but still-standing lighthouse. A detachment of marines and seamen from the *Concord* landed at the light station a short time afterward and found that the Indians had retreated. They also discovered, much to their surprise, that the lighthouse keeper had survived the attack. There he was in the lantern waving at them and calling to them for help. But how to get him down from his high perch?

First the sailors tried to fly a line to Thompson with a kite. When this failed, they tied the line onto a ramrod and fired it up into the lantern with a musket. Employing the last of his strength, Thompson used the line to haul up a tail block, enabling two sailors to pull themselves up to the lantern. They, in turn, lowered Thompson to the ground. Treated for his burns and wounds in a military hospital, Thompson recovered and later continued his service as a lighthouse keeper. Thompson had lived through his worst experience in a Florida lighthouse. Not all Florida keepers would be so fortunate.

ST. AUGUSTINE LIGHT
St. Augustine, Florida - 1821

The Spanish may have built the first lighthouse in Florida, but no one knows for sure. Shortly after the U.S. acquisition of Florida in 1821, the government sent a team of inspectors to examine an old and somewhat mysterious tower near St. Augustine. The inspectors believed the Spanish may have used the three-story structure as a lighthouse. Built by early Spanish settlers near the spot where Ponce de Leon had landed in 1513, the tower stood in a tiny, quarter-acre compound enclosed by walls ten feet high and sixteen inches thick. A small stone building inside the compound may have served as a home, perhaps for a lighthouse keeper.

St. Augustine was the leading port in the new U.S. territory of Florida, and Congress wanted a navigational light established there quickly. Taking for granted that the Spanish tower had, indeed, once served as a lighthouse, the officials ordered a lantern placed atop its third story as a temporary signal for mariners. Plans were made to refurbish the crumbling tower and outfit it with the latest navigational lamps and lens. But after an inspection of the building by St. Augustine customs collector John Rodman, officials decided against using the tower, which was only forty-four feet tall, as a lighthouse. After a careful examination of the

tower, with the help of a mason and a carpenter, Rodman declared the structure unsound and determined that the cost of renovation would soar to at least $5,000. In his report, Rodman said he believed the building was a watchtower and had never been used as a lighthouse.

On orders from Washington, Rodman had a brick tower constructed a little less than 1,000 feet to the southwest of the Spanish compound. Completed in 1824, it rose seventy-three feet above sea level. Partly because it was provided with only a fourth-order lens, which was illuminated with oil lamps intensified by bowl-shaped reflectors, the usefulness of the light was limited to marking the entrance to the St. Augustine harbor.

Like most of the Florida lights, the St. Augustine Lighthouse came under assault by both man and nature. Early in the Civil War, the Confederates darkened it. Then, shortly after it was relit in 1867, the tower was threatened by the sea, as storm-driven erosion brought tides to within just forty-eight feet of its foundation. Consequently, the Lighthouse Board decided to build a new tower on a more secure location about half a mile away on Anastasia Island.

Construction began in 1872, but funds ran out before the brickwork could be carried up more than a few feet. Meanwhile, the sea rapidly closed in on the old lighthouse; water lapped within ten feet at high tide. Hoping to slow the erosion, workers hurriedly laid down a jetty of brush and coquina, a soft limestone composed of shells and coral, and this stopgap measure bought valuable time.

The interruption in funding proved only temporary, and with money flowing again, workers were able to complete the new lighthouse in less than two years; the keeper lit its first-order lens on October 15, 1874. Meanwhile, the sea continued its advance on the old tower, finally enveloping it in 1880.

The new light was more powerful than the old one had been; it had a focal plane 161 feet above the sea and could be seen for nineteen miles. Painted with barber-pole stripes to make it easier to identify during the day, the tower was a near duplicate of others built in the 1870s at Cape Hatteras, Bodie Island, and Currituck Beach.

This is one of the few lighthouses in a populated area. From downtown St. Augustine, take the bridge toward St. Augustine Beach. The lighthouse, with its white and black spiral stripes, is on the left side of the highway.

The Junior League of St. Augustine has restored the keeper's house and opened it as a lighthouse museum. Exhibits in the house tell of the social life of this historic city and of the many famous people who visited the lighthouse. Beautiful live oak trees surround the complex and border the sweeping front yard of the house. It is perhaps the most elegant keeper's quarters in the South, and the restoration and exhibits are among the best in the South.

The tower is not open to the public since the light is still in service. For more information, contact the Junior League of St. Augustine, Box 224, St. Augustine, Florida 32084.

(below) The lighthouse tower overlooks the beautiful St. Augustine Beach.

(above left and right) The sweeping curves of the stairway lead to the light at St. Augustine.

KEY WEST LIGHT
Key West, Florida - 1825

Florida's greatest menace to shipping was its keys, the long chain of low islands curving southwestward from Biscayne Bay. Captains of seventeenth-century Spanish treasure ships called them *Islas de los Martires,* or Islands of Martyrs.

Some say the islands were given their foreboding name because they were covered with scrubby, wind-twisted trees that reminded Spanish sailors of the tortured bodies of Christian martyrs. Others say the islands earned the name by taking the lives of so many seamen.

Ships met with disaster in the keys with such regularity that salvaging their cargoes became a lucrative industry, especially after Florida became a U.S. territory. At first, the American-owned salvage boats, called "wreckers," worked out of foreign ports, such as Havana, since they had no convenient base in American waters. Likewise, the navy had no port to use as a base for operations against the pirates who swarmed through the Keys and the nearby Bahamas. But the navy located a deep-water harbor at Key West and, in 1822, purchased the island from its Spanish owner, Juan Pablo Salas, for $2,000.

Formerly, Key West had been a strong-hold for pirates. Now, almost overnight it grew into a thriving port with a major naval base and large warehouses to store salvaged goods. In 1825 alone almost $300,000 worth of salvage was sold at auction in Key West. That same year the government had a sixty-five-foot lighthouse built on Whitehead Point to mark the entrance to Key West's harbor.

A hurricane swept over Key West in 1846, demolishing much of the town. It also destroyed the lighthouse, killing the keeper along with his entire family. Within a year, workers had replaced the wrecked tower with another about sixty feet tall. A late-nineteenth-century renovation raised the focal plane of the beacon to eighty-five feet above sea level.

Take US-1 south out of Key Largo. This overseas highway runs 100 miles over bridges and keys until it enters Key West and becomes Truman Avenue. The lighthouse, no longer in service, is at the intersection of Truman Avenue and Whitehead Street. The tower is open to the public, and the old military museum next to it now contains lighthouse exhibits. The tower and the museum are open daily (except Christmas Day) from 9:30 A.M. to 5:00 P.M. Admission for adults is $2. For more information, call (305) 294–0012.

CAPE FLORIDA LIGHT
Bill Baggs State Recreation Area, Florida - ca. 1825

Not long after the construction of the Key West Light, a sixty-five-foot lighthouse tower was erected at the opposite (northeastern) end of the island chain. Built in 1825 on Cape Florida, some thirty miles north of Carysfort Reef at the northern entrance to Biscayne Bay, the brick tower had walls five feet thick.

Severely damaged during the 1836 Seminole siege, the lighthouse remained out of service for nearly ten years, largely because the Indians made the site too dangerous for repair crews. When reconstruction was finally underway in 1846, workers discovered that the lighthouse had been the victim not only of Indians but also of fraud. Samuel B. Lincoln, the contractor who had built the tower more than twenty years earlier, had given it hollow walls, saving himself nearly 50 percent on the cost of brick.

The reef-laden coast of southeastern Florida had been claiming ships since the area was discovered in 1497 by John Cabot. And now, even with its light burning again, Cape Florida remained deadly. Ship captains complained that, all too often, they could not see the light. So, following a series of disastrous wrecks during the early 1850s, the board raised the tower to 100 feet above sea level, fitting it with a new Fresnel lens.

Relations with the Seminoles were not always hostile. The Indians regularly traded with the keepers and their families; in fact, they occasionally took the hospitality of the keepers a bit too far. One evening, a Seminole came to the lighthouse keeper to barter. Finding everyone in bed, he slipped into bed himself with one of the children where, to the horror of the keeper's wife, he was found the next morning.

The Cape Florida Light, framed by palms.

During the Civil War, the lighthouse had a new set of enemies, the Confederates, who destroyed the illuminating apparatus in 1861. Restored in 1866, it remained in service another twelve years, after which it was replaced by a new lighthouse at Fowey Rocks, two miles southeast of Key Biscayne. But the story of the Cape Florida Lighthouse did not end there. During the 1970s the Coast Guard decided to refurbish and recommission it. Coincidentally, the old sentinel was relighted in 1978, exactly 100 years after it had been extinguished.

(above left) Living room of reconstructed keeper's residence
(above right) Door of Cape Florida Light that was attacked by Seminole Indians.

Located only a few miles from downtown Miami, this lighthouse is in a tropical setting of coconut palms and Australian pines at the Bill Baggs State Recreation Area. It can be reached by taking the Rickenbacker Causeway at the southern terminus of I-95. Avoid taking the interstate during the rush hour, when the traffic moves at a snail's pace. There is a $1 toll fee to get onto the island and a $1 admission charge to the Bill Baggs Recreation Area.

Once inside the recreation area, it seems impossible that a major city is nearby; thick woods lead down to a white sand beach. The lighthouse is near the parking area for the beach. Both a reconstructed keeper's house and the tower are open to the public for guided tours. The tours are limited to twenty-five people and are offered at 10:30 A.M., 1:00 P.M., 2:30 P.M., and 3:30 P.M.

AMELIA ISLAND LIGHT
Amelia Island, Florida - 1839

In 1820 the government had a sixty-five-foot tower erected on Georgia's Cumberland Island. Its light marked the mouth of the St. Marys River, where it forms a natural border between Georgia and Florida. Following the annexation of Florida as a U.S. territory, the officials decided that the lighthouse would provide better service on the south bank of the river. So, in 1839, Cumberland Lighthouse was dismantled and moved to Amelia Island.

Named for the daughter of King George II of England, Amelia Island was once a swamp, infested not only with mosquitoes but also with pirates, smugglers, and slave traders. Slaves were brought to Amelia and then sold up the St. Marys River by a ring of smugglers known as the Moccasin Boys. These traffickers decoyed their slave-smuggling operations by spreading rumors of Indian attacks. Not surprisingly, they did not care to have other Florida settlers see what they were doing, since theirs was a particularly vile trade. The slaves were transported to Florida in small schooners; as many as 150 naked Africans might be packed into the dark holds of these ships, where many died of infection and exposure. It is said that in 1818 alone, as many as 1,000 slaves were brought to Amelia by the Moccasins and smuggled up the St. Marys.

Eventually, the slave smuggling diminished and was replaced by a vigorous trade in lumber, phosphate, shrimp, and military supplies. During the 1850s Florida's first railroad was laid in, connecting Amelia with Cedar Key on the far side of the state. All this activity brought more ships to the St. Marys and more people to Amelia.

Amelia Island Light is a classical Victorian structure, with a tapering white-washed stone tower and a lantern room as a crown. But the keeper's two-story house, decked with galleries and canopies, reflects the antebellum flavor of the local architecture. Plenty of draped mosquito netting was a necessary feature of the house's interior decor.

The Lighthouse Board had the Amelia Island tower renovated in 1885 and again in the early 1900s, raising the focal plane of the light to 105 feet above mean high water. The tower stands two miles from the north end of the island and one mile from the town of Fernandina.

Fitted with a third-order Fresnel lens, made by Barbier and Bernard of Paris, the light was originally powered by an oil lamp that burned with 1,500 candlepower. It was rotated by a clockwork mechanism that had to be rewound every four hours. Now electrified and automated, the light can be seen from twenty-three miles at sea. Sailors nearing shoals in Nassau Sound see a red flash, while others see a white flash. Amelia Island Light is still on active duty, guiding pleasure craft on the Intracoastal Waterway as well as tankers on the open Atlantic.

The lighthouse is located in a residential section of town on Lighthouse Circle but unfortunately is closed to the public. The only access is across private property posted No Trespassing.

(left) The Amelia Island Light, a classical Victorian structure, was moved to its present site from Cumberland Island, Georgia, in 1839.

CAPE KENNEDY (CANAVERAL) LIGHT

Cape Canaveral Airforce Station - 1848

Sometimes construction of a lighthouse did more harm than good to shipping. In 1848 the government built a lighthouse to warn ships away from a bank of dangerous shoals extending several miles to the east of Florida's Cape Canaveral. But the brick tower was only sixty-five feet tall, and its light was so weak that mariners were already over the shoals before they could see it. Some ships ran aground on the shoals when their captains brought them too close to shore while searching the landward horizon for the Canaveral Light.

In 1859 the Lighthouse Board tried to correct the situation by raising a second, much taller tower at Canaveral. But construction crews had just started on the foundation when the Civil War put a stop to their efforts. At war's end they went back to work, and the new tower was completed by the summer of 1868. A cast-iron cylinder lined with brick, the tower stood 139 feet above sea level, and its light could be seen from eighteen miles at sea, a distance more than sufficient to keep ships away from the Canaveral shoals.

Like many lighthouses built on the shifting sands of the South's Atlantic coast, this second Canaveral tower was eventually threatened by erosion. Engineers fought back against the encroaching ocean with stone jetties, but the tides kept gaining on the lighthouse. In 1893, with waves crashing within 200 feet of the tower foundation, the board had the structure dismantled and rebuilt more than a mile west of its original location.

Since 1964 the Canaveral Light has been known as Cape Kennedy Lighthouse; the name change honors the fallen U.S. president who committed the country to placing a man on the moon before 1970. Sailors still use the old light to navigate safely around the Canaveral shoals, but for decades now they have often seen other bright lights on the cape—rockets rushing skyward from the nearby Kennedy Space Center.

Still an operating lighthouse, this nineteenth-century navigation marker has flashed its beam across the bows of modern vessels with names such as Mercury, Atlas, Gemini, Titan, and Apollo. The Air Force Station is accessible to the public only by bus tours from Kennedy Space Center. From I-95 or US-1, take the NASA Parkway. Turn northeast onto County 3, and follow the signs to the Kennedy Space Center. The bus tour costs $4 for adults. Not all tours pass by the lighthouse. For more information, contact Spaceport USASM, Visitors Center TWS, Kennedy Space Center, Florida 32899; (407) 452–2121.

(right) The Atlas Centaur 9 takes off at Cape Canaveral, within sight of the Cape Kennedy Light.

JUPITER INLET LIGHT
Jupiter, Florida - 1860

A terrible hurricane ripped through Jupiter Inlet in 1928, knocking out the lighthouse's newly installed electrical system. When the station's emergency generator failed to start, the shoreline fell dark just at the time when passing ships most needed guidance. Keeper Charles Seabrook, despite a severely infected hand, reinstalled the light's old mineral lamps but was too weakened by pain to operate them manually. Seabrook's sixteen-year-old son persuaded his father to let him climb the tower, by now an inverted pendulum swaying seventeen inches off-center. The boy proved himself a man as he turned the light by hand and kept it moving for four harrowing hours.

Trouble shrouded the Jupiter Light from the beginning. Angry Seminoles, heat, shallow water, and mosquitoes delayed its lighting for nearly four years after construction started in the late 1850s. Since the inlet was too shallow for navigation at that time, building materials were unloaded from large sailing vessels at Indian River Inlet and lightered the thirty-five miles to Jupiter Inlet in shallow-draft scows. To move the 500 tons of material needed to build the lighthouse, the grueling trek had to be repeated fifty times. The light was finally fired up in July 1860.

The light burned for little more than a year before it was extinguished by Confederate raiders who hoped to impede the movement of blockading Union ships. The men in gray removed and hid the big Fresnel lens. At the end of the Civil War, Captain James A. Armour, who was to enjoy a record forty-year career as keeper of Jupiter Inlet Light, found the lens buried in Jupiter Creek. He had it reinstalled and working by the end of 1866.

At Jupiter Inlet, Armour lived a life even more isolated than that of most other

lighthouse keepers. When he brought his new bride to the inlet in 1867, she was the only white woman for 100 miles.

Although a sign in front of the lighthouse says, It Has Not Missed a Night in Over 100 Years, the light was, in fact, darkened briefly in the 1950s when a hurricane knocked out the windows in the lantern and smashed the irreplaceable bullseye lens. This misfortune might have doomed the light had not technician James Maher painstakingly cemented the shards back into their original configuration and bound them together with a brass framework.

Congress authorized construction of Jupiter Inlet Lighthouse because of the treacherous geology surrounding Jupiter Island, where the Loxahatchee River meets the Atlantic Ocean. A large reef located just offshore is a formidable obstacle to westbound ships needing to cross the Gulf Stream before heading north. The first-order lens, with its focal plane 146 feet above the sea, serves a dual function, warning vessels of the reef and guiding ships along the coast.

George Gordon Meade designed the tower, with its iron latticework frame for the lantern windows and portholes over the lantern gallery. Meade, though best known for defeating General Robert E. Lee in the Battle of Gettysburg, built many of Florida's lighthouses, including the revolutionary screw-pile lights of the Florida Reef.

The Jupiter Inlet Lighthouse has been placed on the National Register of Historic Places. Indeed, it is among the most storied and historic of American lights. The tower itself was built on a prehistoric Indian mound of oyster shells. The route of the Indian River steamer ended at Jupiter, and Florida's famed "Celestial Railroad" began at Jupiter and ran through Mars, Venus, and Juno. A famed lifesaving station was set up at the inlet in 1885 to deal with shipwrecks. A telegraph station was built on the grounds of the lighthouse in 1911. Nearby the lighthouse was a schoolhouse built for the children of Florida's early nineteenth-century pioneers. Many schoolmarms married lighthouse keepers, who were among the few available bachelors. Descendants of these unions still live in the area.

Storms continue to plague the Jupiter coast. In 1872 a powerful gale rolled out of the northeast, driving the steamer *Victor* aground just south of the Jupiter Inlet. The passengers and crew aboard the freighter might never have reached shore without the assistance of the Jupiter Lighthouse keeper. No one was killed, but three dogs were apparently orphaned by the accident. The keeper adopted the dogs, naming them Vic, Storm, and Wreck.

This lighthouse, painted a bright red, can be seen from the US-1 bridge over Jupiter Inlet at Jupiter, north of West Palm Beach. At present, the tower stairs are closed to the public, but the base is open on Sunday afternoons. A small museum near the tower is also open on Sundays and contains some interesting artifacts from the lighthouse. For more information, write to the Loxahatchee Historical Society, 805 North US-1, Jupiter, Florida 33477.

PONCE DE LEON INLET LIGHT
Ponce Inlet, Florida - 1887

The first lighthouse built for Ponce de Leon Inlet, then called Mosquito Inlet, collapsed before its lamps had ever been lit. Oil for the lamps still had not been delivered in 1835 when a storm undermined the tower's foundation. Hostile Seminoles prevented workmen from rescuing the tower from further damage, and it soon toppled over and was left in ruins.

Nearly fifty years later, a new lighthouse was erected, this time on the north side of what is now known as Ponce de Leon Inlet. Constructed in Baltimore and shipped south, the tower is 175 feet tall, making it the second tallest lighthouse on the East Coast. Of course, bringing the huge tower ashore was dangerous work; at

least one man was killed in the effort: Major O. E. Babcock, engineer of the Fifth and Sixth Lighthouse Districts.

Lit in the autumn of 1887, the Ponce de Leon Light helped fill the ninety-five-mile gap between the St. Augustine and Cape Canaveral lights. The red-brick conical tower displayed a flashing white light that could be seen from nineteen miles at sea. Drapes were drawn around the tower's third-order Fresnel lens during the day, to prevent the sun from cracking its prisms or concentrating sunlight and starting fires on the ground. Oil for the remote lighthouse was lightered in small boats and carried by hand to the lantern room, 203 spiraling steps from the ground. Kerosene later replaced oil as a fuel.

This lighthouse served all sorts of traffic, including Bahama-bound, Prohibition-era rumrunners, who often pulled into the inlet at night to avoid trouble on the reefs. It was taken out of service in 1970, however, because the beacon atop the New Smyrna Coast Guard Station made it redundant. The tower stood dormant and vulnerable for two years until it was deeded to the townspeople of Ponce Inlet in 1972. Then, in 1983, the old light was reinstated when a sprouting condominium development at New Smyrna Beach obscured the nearby Coast Guard Station's beacon.

A view form the top of the spiral staircase at the Ponce de Leon Inlet Lighthouse.

Take State A1A south from Daytona Beach (the Atlantic Ocean will be on the left-hand side of the road). At Port Orange, go straight on the paved unnumbered road that continues south through Wilbur-by-the-Sea to Ponce Inlet (the "No Outlet" signs mean you are on the correct road). The tall brick lighthouse will be straight ahead when you near the inlet.

A nonprofit organization has restored and opened a complex of buildings at the lighthouse site. The tower is open and can be climbed. Several of the keeper's houses display lighthouse exhibits, and as a group they form one of the best lighthouse museums on the entire East Coast.

The complex is open during daylight hours, and admission is $2. For additional information, contact Ponce de Leon Inlet Lighthouse Museum, 4931 South Peninsula Drive, Ponce Inlet, Florida 32019; (904) 767–3425 or (904) 761–1821.

OLD PORT BOCA GRANDE LIGHT
AND GASPARILLA REAR RANGE LIGHT
Gasparilla Island, Florida - 1890 and 1927

Built in 1890 on Gasparilla Island, Old Port Boca Grande Lighthouse lights the southern stretches of the Florida coast and, some say, marks the grave of a headless Spanish princess. The island is named for José Gaspar, a bloodthirsty pirate with a lusty appetite for gold, silver, and beautiful women. Gaspar's raids on merchant ships netted him many female prisoners, whom he kept on Gasparilla, which he called *Cautiva,* meaning "captive woman."

Gasparilla Island Rear Range Lighthouse

One of Gaspar's captives, a beautiful Spanish princess named Josefa, turned the tables on the pirate by imprisoning his heart. Gaspar was so stricken with the lady that he begged her to marry him. However, the proud Josefa answered his marriage plea with a curse and spat in his eye. In a fit of rage, the pirate drew his saber and beheaded her. Overwhelmed with remorse, Gaspar buried Josefa's body on the beach where he had murdered her. To remind him of his love for the princess, he kept her head in a jar on his ship. It is said that Josefa's decapitated ghost still walks the island in search of its missing head.

Boca Grande Lighthouse sits on iron stilts above the erosive surf near the mouth of Charlotte Harbor. The lighthouse was abandoned by the U.S. Coast Guard in 1967 and quickly became prey for vandals and the elements. In an effort to preserve it, local residents had the lighthouse transferred from federal to local ownership in 1972. In 1980 it was placed on the National Register of Historic Places.

The Gasparilla Island Conservation and Improvement Association began restoring Boca Grande Light in late 1985, with grants from the Bureau of Historic Preservation, the Florida Department of State, and the Historic Preservation Advisory Council. As part of this effort, the Coast Guard reinstalled Boca Grande's crown—the original imported French Fresnel lens—and on November 21, 1986, the old lighthouse was ceremoniously relit for active federal service to navigation. Work continues on the interior, with plans for both an office for the Department of Natural Resources' resident ranger and a local maritime museum.

The iron-pile Gasparilla Island Rear Range Lighthouse, built to the north of Boca Grande Light in 1927, still guides harbor traffic at night. The term *rear range* refers to twin lights, the rear elevated above the front. When a ship can see one directly above the other, the vessel is in mid-channel.

Old Port Boca Grande Light, Florida

To reach Gasparilla Island, take US-41 to Port Charlotte; turn south onto State 776. Just beyond Gulf Cove, take State 771 to Placida, and follow the signs to the toll bridge leading to the island. Once on the island, take the paved road south through the village of Boca Grande. The gulf and the lighthouse will be on the right-hand side of the road. The lighthouse is not open to the public, but there is a special reward for stopping here—a little public beach offering some of the best shelling anywhere on the gulf.

About one mile beyond the Rear Range Light is Old Boca Grande Light, also known as Gasparilla Island Lighthouse. Located in the Florida State Recreation Area at the south end of the island, the lighthouse is not open to the public.

For more information, contact the Gasparilla Island Conservation and Improvement Association, Box 446, Boca Grande, Florida 33921; (813) 964–2667.

HILLSBORO INLET LIGHT
Hillsboro Inlet, Florida - 1906 or 1907

The Hillsboro Inlet Lighthouse was not built in Florida but rather, in the Midwest. Constructed by a Chicago company at a cost of $90,000, it was shipped down the Mississippi to St. Louis, where it delighted crowds at the 1904 Exposition. When the Exposition closed, the lighthouse seemed very out of place. Eventually, it was purchased by the government and moved to Hillsboro Inlet, where it began service as a navigational light in 1907. The last beach lighthouse erected in Florida, it marks the northern approaches to Miami.

The lighthouse was anchored by six huge iron piles, a design innovation intended to ease the strain of wind and water on the structure. The lower third of the octagonal pyramid skeleton was painted white and the upper two-thirds painted black, distinguishing it from its red-brick counterparts at Jupiter Inlet and Cape Florida.

At first, the light was fueled by kerosene, which had to be carried by keepers up the 175 steps in the central stair cylinder to the lantern room, 136 feet above mean sea level. The lens rotated on a mercury-filled reservoir and was driven by a clockwork mechanism powered by a weight. The keeper had to raise the weight by hand every half hour.

The light was converted to electric power in the late 1920s and in 1966 was upgraded to 2,000,000 candlepower. The lens makes one complete revolution

The Hillsboro Inlet Lighthouse was displayed at the 1904 Exposition in St. Louis.

every forty seconds, with one-second flashes every twenty seconds. Its light can be seen from twenty-five miles away.

During the light's early years, a series of unexplained fires broke out in the area near the tower. After much investigation, it was discovered that the fires had been ignited by sunlight concentrated by the powerful lens. To solve this problem, a shield was constructed on the landward side.

A plaque near the lighthouse commemorates the death of James E. Hamilton, the legendary mailman who walked barefoot on his delivery route from Jupiter Light to Miami. Hamilton drowned in 1887 while trying to bring mail across Hillsboro Inlet.

Hillsboro Inlet, named for the Earl of Hillsboro, who surveyed much of Florida during the 1700s, has been a target for many severe storms and hurricanes. But the lighthouse, with its sturdy pile legs, has stood firm. During the 1960s it successfully weathered Hurricane Donna, which sent a massive tidal surge swirling over the dunes and inundating the lighthouse's base.

Statue of James E. Hamilton, the barefoot mailman who walked his delivery route from Jupiter Light to Miami. He is thus commemorated because he drowned trying to bring mail across the Hillsboro Inlet.

This lighthouse is located on State A1A between Pompano Beach and Boca Raton. Still in operation and maintained by the Coast Guard, it is not open to the public, but the tower can be viewed from the State A1A bridge over the inlet. An even better view can be had from the beach on the south side of the inlet.

CHAPTER FOUR

LIGHTS OF HURRICANE ALLEY

Florida Panhandle, Alabama, Mississippi, Louisiana, and Texas

Lights of Hurricane Alley

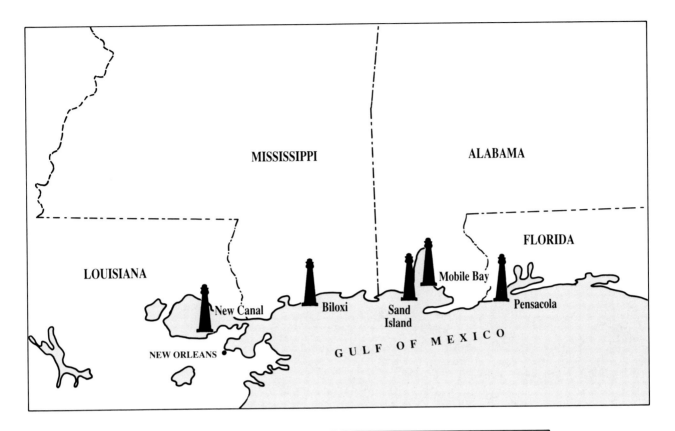

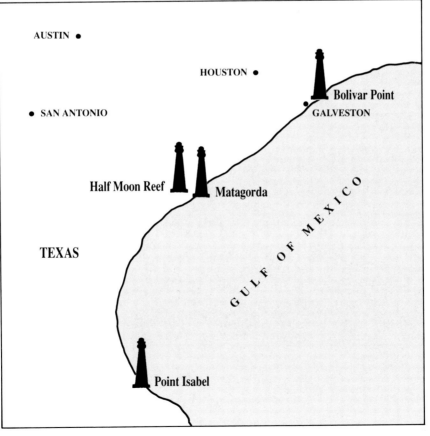

Standing in the gallery of his Bolivar Point Lighthouse on the afternoon of September 7, 1900, keeper Harry Claiborne could see clear signs that trouble was on the way. From his high perch, more than 100 feet above the entrance to Galveston Bay, Claiborne looked down on pristine Texas beaches where, on most days, the blue-green Gulf of Mexico wallowed lazily in the sand. But now the mood of the gulf had changed dramatically. Its waters had turned gray and angry, and it pounded the dunes with enormous waves.

Earlier in the week, when Claiborne had gone into the nearby resort town of Galveston to buy a month's supply of groceries, there was already a hint of uneasiness in people's faces. All summer long the hot, humid air of Galveston Island had buzzed with mosquitoes, but now it vibrated with tension. The weather station on the island had received a distressing cable. Trinidad, on the far side of the Caribbean, had been devastated by a hurricane so powerful that few structures were left standing. It was impossible to say where this deadly storm was now, but sailors arriving at Galveston's bustling wharves brought still more troubling news; they told dock workers, saloon keepers, ladies of the night, and anyone who would listen that they had come through "hell" out in the gulf. Somewhere out there lurked a killer hurricane.

At the turn of the century, meteorologists had no radar or computer-enhanced satellite photos to help them track weather systems; there was no telling where a big storm like this would strike next. It might drift to the east and vent its fury in the empty Atlantic. More likely, however, it would rush northward out of the Caribbean and into the Gulf of Mexico, following a well-traveled path known to sailors as "hurricane alley." In that case, it would threaten all the gulf states from Florida to Texas.

Chances were slim that the storm would hit any one stretch of coastline, so the people of Galveston had no immediate cause for alarm. But then the wind picked up, and high, wispy clouds shaped like fish scales were seen racing westward over the island. The atmospheric pressure started dropping so fast that the barometer at the Galveston Weather Station seemed to have sprung a leak. Seeing these rapid changes, the Weather Bureau put out an emergency forecast—just one word—and editors of the local paper set that word in very large type for their morning editions: HURRICANE.

Strangely, most people ignored the warning. Some even rode out to the island on excursion trains from Houston to witness the natural spectacle firsthand. Throughout the morning of September 8, larger and larger crowds gathered to watch the huge waves slamming into the Galveston beaches. Children squealed with delight and clapped their hands as the big waves crashed down, throwing frothy spray into their faces. It was a tremendous show.

Seeing the big crowd of spectators gathered on the shore, Weather Bureau meteorologist Isaac Cline could not believe his eyes. Was it possible that these fools were ignorant of the imminent danger they faced? Cline knew hurricanes often generated tides of a dozen feet or more; the town was only eight feet above sea level. It required very little mathematical skill to deduce that a really powerful storm could wash right over Galveston Island and drown everyone on it.

Cline drove up and down the beach in a horse-drawn buggy, shouting at people to go home or, if they could, to get to the mainland. Few listened to him. The twentieth century had arrived, bringing with it trains, steamships, electric lights, and bottled soda. Why should anyone fear a summer storm? Desperately, Cline pointed to the hurricane flags cracking like whips in the wind. But few noticed the flags, even when the gale started ripping them to tatters.

The revelers at the beach would not listen to the plea of a weatherman, but the weather itself soon confronted them with a more forceful argument. A wooden pagodalike structure stretched several hundred feet along a two-block stretch of the Galveston beach. It was used on holidays and weekends as a dance floor and as a boardwalk for strolling lovers. But now the surf was using it as a punching bag. The pagoda began to sag, and within minutes, the waves turned it into a surging mass of driftwood. This calamity finally convinced people that the approaching storm meant business. Much to Cline's relief, the crowd of wave-watchers began to disperse. Those who lived nearby hurried home and nailed up their shutters. Others began to look for ways to get off the island. But for many it was already too late.

At Bolivar Point, Claiborne made sure his light had plenty of oil. Its beacon would be needed by ships caught in the storm and seeking haven in the calmer waters of Galveston Bay. The keeper did not know it yet, but the lighthouse itself would soon become a haven for scores of terrified people struggling to keep their heads above a boiling flood tide.

A prosperous seaport and resort, turn-of-the-century Galveston had its share of turreted Victorian palaces. Surrounded by tall palms and oleanders, they lined the handsome boulevards that ran down the spine of the island. But only a few of Galveston's 40,000 residents lived in mansions. Most made do in rundown tenements and shacks clustered on the low, marshy ground near the wharves. It was the poor who first felt the murky flood waters swirling around their ankles. Forced to abandon their meager belongings, they fled toward the center of the island, where the homes of the rich stood on slightly higher ground. But the relentless tide followed, and soon, there was no longer any spot on the island that could rightly be described as dry land. Dozens drowned, then hundreds, then thousands.

The high water was not the only danger. The wind hurled boards, beach chairs, and massive tree limbs through the air. It turned pebbles into bullets and shards of broken glass into daggers. It ripped the red-brick tiles from the roofs of public buildings and sent them spinning through the streets to decapitate or crush the skulls of its hapless victims. To be out in the open meant death.

Driven from his house by the rising water, Claiborne sought safety within the strong brick walls of his lighthouse. But he had barely closed the heavy metal door behind him when people started pounding on it, begging him to let them in. Despite the gale and the fast-rising water now covering the floor of the lighthouse, Claiborne shoved open the door; after all, he was in the business of saving lives.

Before long, the tower was crammed all the way to the top with frightened men, women, and children, who clung desperately to the steps and rails of its spiral

Galveston Jetty Lighthouse, Galveston, Texas (Texas US Coast Guard photo)

staircase. More than 100 people, many of them from a train that had been stranded by the flood, found sanctuary in the lighthouse; Claiborne must have wondered how he could fit in any more refugees. After a while, though, no one else came. In fact, the big door was soon hidden under as much as thirty feet of water.

To save themselves from drowning, people on the lower steps had to clamber over the heads and shoulders of those above. Terror-filled voices cried out in the near-total darkness; some called the names of loved ones, hoping that they, too, were safe somewhere above or below on the steps of the tower.

As the hours passed and the storm continued to rage, the air inside the lighthouse grew stifling and fetid. Muscles and limbs became so cramped that people screamed with pain. Some grew ill and threw up on the heads of those below. But no matter how miserable they were, no matter how awful conditions inside became, no one doubted that things were much worse outside. The wind howled and whistled, blasting the tower at speeds of up to 150 miles per hour. Swept along by the flood, the trunks of fallen trees slammed like battering rams into the walls. The tower shook and the staircase quivered, but the old walls, built in 1871, held fast.

People outside the tower snatched safety wherever they could find it, often in the unlikeliest of places. Some climbed palms and clung to the fronds while the wind clawed at them hour after hour. Others grasped the girders of bridges that had been only partially demolished and pulled themselves up out of the flood. Still others hung onto floating boxes and timbers.

Some of the city's solidly built stone mansions stood up to the storm. Pressed together in the upper rooms of these fine old homes were bank presidents and black gardeners, wealthy matrons and Chinese sailors, debutantes and muscular Latin stevedores. The hurricane had blown away all traces of social distinction.

In the heart of the city, a "lighthouse" very different from the one at Bolivar Point also became a refuge from the storm. A high brick wall surrounding Galveston's Ursuline Convent served as a kind of dike to hold back the flood. Nuns pulled scores of helpless storm victims out of the torrent and over the wall to safety. Among those rescued by the nuns was a pregnant woman who had survived by using an empty steamer trunk as a boat. That night in the convent, the woman gave birth to a baby boy who, though he saw nothing of it, had just lived through the greatest adventure of his life.

Sometime during the early morning hours of September 9, the hurricane passed inland toward the dry plains of west Texas, where it dumped the last of its prodigious rains. Having dwindled down to little more than an ordinary thunderstorm, it wreaked no further havoc other than to flood a few gullies and teach a number of lizards and horned toads to swim. But the storm had already done far more than its quota of damage at Galveston.

When the waters had receded sufficiently that the refugees at Bolivar Point could escape their lighthouse prison, they pushed through the tower door into the sunlight. At last, they could breathe and stretch their tortured limbs. But they took no joy in their freedom. Confronted by a scene of utter desolation, they huddled together in horrified silence. Buildings had been knocked down, homes flattened, bridges smashed, ships capsized, trains swept off their tracks, entire communities obliterated. But the most shocking sight of all was right there beside them, just outside the door. Piled up around the base of the lighthouse lay dozens of bodies, many of them stripped naked by the flood. It was as if the tower had been a huge tree, and all these unfortunate people had tried desperately to climb it and keep their heads above the flood. They had failed.

Similar piles of bodies could be seen everywhere throughout the ruins of what once had been the bustling city of Galveston. At least 8,000 people were killed by the storm and the flood tide that accompanied it, but many more may have died. The exact number of dead will never be known.

Even after the storm had passed, the survivors still faced much suffering and hardship. The hurricane had knocked down the bridges and washed away the causeways linking Galveston to the mainland. There were no boats; every vessel in the harbor from the largest freighter to the smallest dinghy had been wrecked or sunk. Cut off from the outside world, the city was without fuel, without sanitation, and without medical facilities of any sort. People could find no food, no shelter, and no unpolluted water to drink. And worst of all, something had to be done with all those bodies.

At Bolivar Point, Claiborne fed and sheltered as best he could the people who had weathered the storm with him in the lighthouse. He quickly exhausted the month's allotment of groceries he had purchased only a few days earlier. He figured he'd get by somehow.

On the evening after the hurricane Claiborne trudged up the steps of the tower. By this time he was no doubt approaching total exhaustion, but duty required that he start up his light and make sure it had plenty of oil. For crews on the battered ships that had ridden out the storm in the Gulf, the Bolivar Point Light was a welcome sight. It was also a comfort to the citizens of Galveston, who had endured so much during the previous forty-eight hours. Each time the beacon flashed, they were reminded that some things, at least, still worked and that even in the darkest hours, a few safe havens remained.

STORM-DASHED SENTINELS: GUARDING THE GULF COAST

Stories about the Gulf Coast lighthouses and the storms that have swept over them go back hundreds of years. In 1699 the French established a settlement at the mouth of the Mississippi River, naming it "The Balize," after a French word that means *beacon* or *seamark*. If the French already had a light shining from The Balize at that time, then it predated by more than a dozen years the 1716 Boston Lighthouse thought by most historians to have been the first such structure in North America. In any case, records confirm that a tower was built at The Balize as early as 1721 by the architect Adrien de Pauger, the same man who designed the city plan for New Orleans. When the Spanish took control of Louisiana in 1762, they began construction of a 120-foot pyramid at The Balize, completing it five years later. Gulf storms no doubt extinguished the beacons atop both the French and Spanish structures on many occasions, but they were always relighted.

During the first half of the nineteenth century, the U.S. government embarked on an extensive program of lighthouse construction along the northern and western Gulf Coast. The Coast Guard built five lighthouses in 1831 alone and eight more during the years 1837–39. By the outbreak of the Civil War, at least fifty-nine towers had been erected, but they were never all in use at the same time. Over the years, each of them was repeatedly blasted by hurricanes and other tropical storms only slightly less destructive. Many of the lighthouses, their foundations undermined by flood tides or their towers knocked down by the wind, had to be rebuilt or replaced several times.

Yet the Civil War, a storm of human making, took a higher toll of lighthouses than any hurricane in history. Union ships fired cannonballs into them, while Confederate artillery pounded them to keep the Northerners from using them as observation posts. Since the Southern Navy was very small, safe navigation mostly benefited the North. So the Confederates removed lighthouse lenses and other equipment and hid them away, plunging most of the Southern coast into darkness. Cast-iron towers were often melted down by the metal-hungry Southerners and reforged to make rifle barrels and cannon shot. But like a natural storm, the war eventually passed, and within a few years most of the Gulf Coast lighthouses were back in business, warning sailors of danger or guiding them to safe harbor.

Of the more than sixty major lighthouses that once stood on the flat, sandy headlands along the thousand miles of coastline from the Florida panhandle to the Mexican border, only a few still function. Many are "darkhouses" now, their lights extinguished and replaced by less costly navigational markers. Some are in ruins, and others have disappeared completely, all traces of them having been erased by the wind and sea. Still, dozens of the old towers remain, much to the delight of architects, historians, and the droves of more casual visitors like ourselves for whom a stretch of shore without a lighthouse is like a beach without the sun.

Stairs of keeper's quarters, St. Augustine, Florida

PENSACOLA LIGHT
Pensacola, Florida - 1824

Following the acquisition of Florida from Spain in 1819, the U.S. naval presence in the Gulf of Mexico increased dramatically. American warships cruised the dark, sparsely settled coast, discouraging smugglers and flushing out nests of pirates. But with their nearest base on the Eastern Seaboard, literally thousands of sea miles away, these fighting ships and their crews might as well have been operating in foreign waters. In 1824 the U.S. Navy moved to remedy this situation by establishing its first Gulf Coast deep-water base at Pensacola. That same year, a lighthouse was erected to guide warships in and out of Pensacola's excellent harbor, which, with thirty-six feet of water, was one of the deepest on the gulf.

The lighthouse tower was only forty feet tall, but it stood on a forty-foot bluff, giving it an effective height of eighty feet. Even so, sea captains frequently complained that the beam was obscured by tall trees. And the light itself was weak; in 1851 congressional investigators found it "deficient in power, being fitted only with ten lamps and sixteen-inch reflectors." These inadequacies made it little more useful than a small harbor light.

The commandant of the Pensacola Naval Station repeatedly urged Congress to provide the harbor with a "first-class seacoast light." Finally, in 1858, he got his wish. A massive brick tower, built at a cost of nearly $25,000, raised the lantern 210 feet above the sea so that its beacon could be seen up to twenty-one miles at sea.

Only a few years after its construction, the big tower became a target for Union gunners firing on Confederate artillerymen dug in around the lighthouse. Unable to keep the lighthouse out of Union hands, the men in gray resorted to the tactic of stealing the lens and apparatus. These were hidden and not found until after the war.

The tower has also withstood bombardment by nature. It has been struck countless times by lightning; in 1875 a pair of bolts seared the lantern, melting and fusing metal parts in the apparatus. Ten years later an earthquake shook the

During the Civil War, the Confederates stole the Pensacola Light's lens and apparatus to incapacitate the Union-occupied light.

structure so hard that the keeper imagined "people were ascending the steps, making as much noise as possible."

Despite the poundings it has taken, the Pensacola Lighthouse still stands. With its bottom third painted white and its top two-thirds painted black, the tower looks much as it has for more than 100 years. Its light, now automated, continues to lead navy ships and Coast Guard cutters into Pensacola Harbor.

The lighthouse, located at the Pensacola Naval Air Station, can be reached by taking Navy Boulevard (State 295) south out of Pensacola. The station is an open post, and the guard at the gate can provide a car pass and directions to the lighthouse. Although the tower and the keeper's quarters are not open to the public, visitors can tour the grounds. The lighthouse complex has several other buildings, which were used to store lamp oil and supplies. The complex is in remarkably good condition, probably because it has been protected on the base and maintained by the navy.

The old keeper's quarters have been converted into Lighthouse Apartments and can be rented on a daily basis. For information, write to the Lighthouse Apartments, Oak Grove Park, Naval Air Station, Pensacola, Florida 32508.

The first-order lens which illuminates the Pensacola Light

ST. MARKS LIGHT
St. Marks, Florida - 1831

Florida history buffs like to argue that the first lighthouse in North America stood on the banks of the St. Marks River near the point where their state begins to bend westward into its panhandle. They make the rather intriguing assertion that the Spanish, during their early explorations, raised a light at the mouth of the river. But like those who claim priority for the French light at The Balize in Louisiana, they can cite no decisive evidence; the Boston Harbor Light, built in 1716, remains generally recognized as America's first lighthouse.

The old Spanish light, if it ever existed at all, was gone by the early eighteenth century, when control of the area passed from Spain to the United States. But officials in Washington soon recognized the commercial importance of the Spanish settlement at St. Marks, and in 1828 Congress appropriated $6,000 for a light to mark the entrance of the harbor. The builders must have been the ancestors of some of today's government contractors; they scrimped on materials to such an extent that the walls were actually left hollow. In fact, their work was so shoddy that the tower had to be demolished, lest it fall down of its own accord and hurt somebody.

The new, solid-walled tower erected in its place was well constructed, but the masons who built it might as well have saved themselves the sweat. The river quickly undercut its foundations, forcing the government to pull it down yet again and rebuild it on another, safer location.

This third tower was truly a fine piece of work and raised the lantern to a point

Despite Confederate attempts to blow up the St. Marks Light during the Civil War, the light was restored and remains a landmark today.

seventy-three feet above sea level. From this height its fifteen lamps and fifteen-inch reflectors enabled it to be seen by ships more than a dozen miles at sea. The brick-and-mortar tower still stands, despite the violence to which nature and man have subjected it.

During the Seminole Indian Wars, a nervous keeper pleaded for an army detachment to protect the light station—and his scalp. His superiors ignored him and, luckily, so did the rebellious Seminoles. But when the Civil War broke out, the rebels in gray did not ignore the lighthouse. Fearing it would be used to guide Union ships into the strategic St. Marks Harbor, Confederate soldiers tried to blow it up with kegs of gunpowder stacked inside the tower. The blast knocked out a full third of its circumference, but the stubborn tower put on a superb balancing act and refused to fall. Shortly after the war, the Lighthouse Board managed to repair the lighthouse and by early 1867, had it back in service.

The St. Marks Lighthouse is no longer in use, but it still stands and remains among the most picturesque sights on the Gulf Coast. Located in a pristine refuge, alive with sea birds and other wildlife, it is well worth a visit.

Located in the St. Marks National Wildlife Refuge, the lighthouse can be reached by taking State 363 from Tallahassee to St. Marks. Follow signs to the wildlife refuge and take the paved highway through the refuge to the shore of the Gulf of Mexico. The large parking area serves bird-watchers, beach users, and lighthouse visitors.

Even though the tower and keeper's house are not open to the public, it is well worth the trip to see this lighthouse, probably the most photographed lighthouse on the Gulf Coast. Birds and alligators abound in the swamps surrounding the lighthouse. Bring your camera.

CAPE ST. GEORGE LIGHT

St. George Island, Florida - 1833

The seventy-foot lighthouse tower on St. George Island had stood for only a few years when a storm came blasting out of the gulf and knocked it down. Rebuilt in 1852, the tower was fitted with a third-order lens that made the light visible more than fifteen miles at sea. This second tower proved much stronger or, perhaps, luckier than the first; it still stands today, despite repeated assaults by hurricanes, gales, and Confederate guns.

During the Civil War, the Confederates fired on the lighthouse and managed to put it out of service temporarily. But the damage was repaired and the light back in use again by the time the war ended in 1865. Not until 1889 did keepers notice a dark, angular crack in the lens, apparently put there by a well-aimed rebel shot.

Marking the western entrance to the Apalachicola Bay, the Cape St. George Lighthouse is in use today. Located on an isolated and uninhabited island, the automated light operates on battery power. The keeper's house and other outbuildings are in ruins, but the tower itself remains as tall and lovely as ever. The island is a fine place to hunt for seashells or, if you like, to be alone for a while.

This isolated lighthouse stands on a remote island which can only be reached by boat. Since the island is not inhabited, visitors should take along drinking water and food. For information and advice on transportation, write the Apalachicola Bay Chamber of Commerce, 45 Market Street, Apalachicola, Florida 32320.

The Cape St. George Light still stands, despite repeated assaults upon it by nature and man.

97

CAPE SAN BLAS LIGHT
Cape San Blas, Florida - 1847

A few miles west of the Apalachicola River, the Florida panhandle juts out into the gulf. Here, sand and silt churned up by swirling currents have formed an angular navigational obstacle called Cape San Blas. The same natural process that built the cape also created a series of dangerous shoals extending four to five miles out into the gulf. Constantly shifting and frequently raked by powerful storms, the shoals are a sailor's nightmare. Keeping a light on the cape to warn away ships has likewise proved a nightmare for lighthouse officials.

The Cape San Blas Lighthouse had stood for only four years when, in 1851, it fell in a hurricane—the same giant storm that knocked down the tower at Cape St. George. It took fever-plagued construction crews five years to rebuild the San Blas tower, but its light had shown for only a few months when a gale pushed it over again.

Undeterred, the Lighthouse Board put crews to work once more and had the light back in operation just in time for the Civil War. Confederate raiders hit the cape almost as hard as a hurricane, burning down the keeper's house and torching everything combustible—even the doors and window sashes in the lighthouse tower.

Relighted after the war, the light was in trouble again by the late 1870s. This time the threat was erosion—the gulf was eating away the cape. By 1880 the surf had reached the base of the lighthouse, and within two years the tower stood in eight feet of water. Its foundation undermined by seawater, the tower began to settle, leaning further toward the

The Cape San Blas Light's iron tower was erected in 1885 after it was salvaged from a ship that had sunk.

gulf each day. Finally, it could no longer keep its balance and crashed down into the waves.

The board now made plans for yet another lighthouse at Cape San Blas, this one of a type far less susceptible to high winds and water. Instead of a brick-and-mortar tower, it would have a lightweight iron skeleton held together by struts and wires. While the skeleton was under construction at a shipyard in the North, a small light placed on the end of a long pole did the work of alerting ships' crews to the danger of the shoals. This makeshift arrangement continued for longer than anyone had expected, since the ship ferrying the prefabricated skeleton to the gulf sank near Sanibel Island, south of Tampa Bay.

Somehow, the board managed to salvage its iron tower and by 1885 had it in place about 500 feet from the beach on Cape San Blas. But the gulf continued its landward march, often chewing up the cape at the astounding rate of one foot each day. The light had to be moved twice more; eventually the gulf forced the board to move the tower almost a quarter of a mile north.

Located on the Cape San Blas Coast Guard Station, the light is still in use. Visitors who don't mind climbing to the top of the ninety-foot tower can see cracks said to be made by Confederate musket balls in the revolving Fresnel lens.

Take US-98 west from Apalachicola. After about six miles, turn left onto State 30/22 and drive through McNeils (the road becomes State 30E). Follow 30E for roughly four miles until it curves sharply to the right; there take an unmarked dirt road straight ahead several hundred yards to the lighthouse. For more information, contact the Apalachicola Bay Chamber of Commerce, 45 Market Street, Apalachicola, Florida 32320.

Since its construction in 1885, the San Blas Light's tower has been moved three times to evade the Gulf of Mexico's erosion upon the shore.

CROOKED RIVER LIGHT
Carrabelle, Florida - 1895

As early as 1838 a small, isolated light station operated on windy Dog Island, a few miles south of Carrabelle, Florida. For decades, lights there guided freighters into the mouth of the aptly named Crooked River, where they took on valuable loads of hardwood lumber. Then, one day in the fall of 1873, the station keeper looked out into the gulf and saw a mass of black clouds rushing at him from the south. This was no mere gale but a hurricane packing killer winds and a floodtide that soon put the entire island under water. The storm swept the low, sandy island clean, dumping the lighthouse, the keeper's dwelling, and, probably, the keeper himself into the sea. Following this disaster, the board decided not to rebuild the Dog Island Lighthouse.

Lumber boats and freighters, however, continued to pay frequent visits to Carrabelle. By the 1880s this traffic had increased dramatically; and since the Crooked River had a deep entrance, with some eighteen feet of water at the bar, officials saw potential here for a large port. So the board made plans to replace the wrecked Dog Island Light with a mainland lighthouse to be built near the mouth of the river.

In 1889, the board sought and received $40,000 from Congress to construct a skeleton-style iron tower on the banks of the Crooked River, but the money was not put to use until nearly five years later. Confusion over title to the land and other delays kept workmen away from the construction site until late in 1894. Once underway, though, work progressed so swiftly that the lantern and fixtures were in place by October 1895.

The tower lifted the lantern's fourth-order lens 115 feet above sea level, high enough for the light to be seen from sixteen miles away. The revolving lens showed two flashes every ten seconds. The Crooked River Lighthouse, its lower half painted white and upper half painted dark red, remains in use today.

The lighthouse can be seen from US-98, a few miles west of Carrabelle. A dirt road leads to the tower, located a few hundred yards off the highway. The tower is not open to the public, and there are no facilities of any kind.

SAND ISLAND LIGHT
Mobile Bay, Alabama - 1838

The island for which this lighthouse was named no longer exists and, for that matter, neither does the light itself. The island long ago eroded and washed away, but the light was extinguished only recently—by a flood of modern shipboard navigational aids that made it unnecessary. Abandoned, isolated, and completely surrounded by the inky waters of Mobile Bay, the black Sand Island tower stands today only as a monument to its own violent and tragic past.

A fifty-five-foot tower was raised on the island in 1838 as a complement to the Mobile Point Light on the opposite side of the entrance to Mobile Bay. Relatively small for a coastal lighthouse, it eventually proved unequal to its task, and plans were made to erect a much larger structure in its place. When completed in 1859, at a cost of $35,000, the new, 150-foot tower was crowned with a first-order lens that probably made the light visible from more than twenty miles at sea.

But the big lighthouse stood for only two years. In 1861 Confederate soldiers noticed Union spotters using the lighthouse to spy on their gun emplacements at Fort Morgan. Under cover of darkness, a rebel raiding party rowed out to the island and blew up the tower, toppling it into the bay.

After the lighthouse was rebuilt during 1871–72 by a yellow fever–tormented work crew, the island beneath the structure began to erode. By 1896 the island beneath Alabama's first and only coastal lighthouse had completely disappeared. During the next ten years, the island reappeared several times, only to vanish in the next storm. Then, in 1906, a hurricane washed it away forever.

Unfortunately, the storm carried away more than just the sand. After the hurricane had passed inland and the winds had died down, a worried lighthouse inspector hurried out to check on the Sand Island Light station and its keepers. Later, the inspector sent this telegram to his superiors: "Sand Island Light out. Island washed away. Dwelling gone. Keepers not to be found."

Although its light has been extinguished and the island it stands on is inundated, this storm-battered tower still stands. Surrounded by water, it can only be reached by boat. Dauphin Island, the closest place to launch a boat, can be reached by driving south from Mobile on State 163.

Abandoned and isolated, Sand Island Light's black tower stands alone in Mobile Bay.

MOBILE BAY LIGHT
Mobile Bay, Alabama - 1885

Built in a style used frequently in the Chesapeake Bay, the Mobile Bay Lighthouse consists of a hexagon-shaped cottage with a lantern perched atop its roof. The structure rests on iron pilings screwed into the muddy floor of the bay.

Although quite similar in style, the Mobile Bay Lighthouse proved much more difficult to build than its cousins in the Chesapeake. The iron skeleton that was to hold the lighthouse above the shallow waters of the bay was prefabricated in the North and shipped by sea to Alabama without incident. The trouble began when crews had to erect the skeleton on its pilings far out in the bay. Located in very middle of the bay, the construction site was exposed to the worst weather the gulf could throw at it. Gales hindered crews, and on more than one occasion workmen had to flee for their lives to the Alabama mainland.

While still under construction, the lighthouse began to sink into the sticky mud at the bottom of the bay. Before long, it had lost more than seven feet of its height; but since the settling was evenly distributed, the structure remained sound. The board ordered the light placed in service, and it first shined on December 1, 1885, displaying a white light with red flashes every thirty seconds.

Although five additional lighthouses were planned to mark the serpentine channels through the bay, no more were built. The original cottage lighthouse has stood now for more than a century, a lone sentinel at the heart of Mobile Bay. Although its lamp has been extinguished for many years, ships continue to use the Mobile Bay Lighthouse as a daymark. The Coast Guard intended to demolish the structure in 1967, but spirited public opposition prevented its removal.

Located in the harbor, the lighthouse can only be reached by boat. It is still used as a daymark for ship traffic in and out of Mobile.

Although inoperable for many years, the Mobile Bay Light is still a decorative addition to Alabama's coast.

BILOXI LIGHT
Biloxi, Mississippi - 1848

Often located on empty barrier islands or remote spits of sand, lighthouses are frequently isolated and hard to reach. Not so the Biloxi Light. Its white, forty-eight-foot tower sits sandwiched between the eastbound and westbound lanes of U.S. Highway 90.

The brick-and-mortar tower is sheathed in a cast-iron shell. This design has proved a successful one and has enabled the tower to survive countless gulf storms, including the infamous Hurricane Camille in 1968.

In the late 1860s the tower was painted black, and legend has it that this was done as a sign of mourning for President Lincoln. It is an unlikely story, especially when one considers that from the tower you can see Beauvoir, the home of Jefferson Davis who, as president of the Confederacy, was Lincoln's most implacable enemy.

After the Civil War, beach erosion threatened the lighthouse, causing it to lean a full two feet off the perpendicular. In a desperate attempt to save the structure, workers excavated soil from beneath the tower on the side away from the lean. Almost miraculously, their fight to save the tower succeeded, and it settled back into plumb.

For more than half a century, the Biloxi Lighthouse was kept by a woman. Maria Youghans became keeper in 1867 and only retired in 1920—when her daughter took over the job.

This lighthouse stands in the median strip of US-90 at the foot of Porter Avenue in Biloxi. It is the only lighthouse in the South located on a major highway, and it's right in the middle of it—a marker for motorists as well as seamen.

The light is still maintained by the Coast Guard, although the tower is now owned by the city of Biloxi. The lighthouse is open to the public from May to September on Saturdays and Sundays, 10:00 a.m. to 4:00 p.m. It is open other times by appointment; call (601) 374–8600, ext. 351.

The Biloxi Light stands within sight of Beauvoir, Jefferson Davis' home as president of the Confederacy.

NEW CANAL LIGHT
New Orleans, Louisiana - 1838

One of a series of inland lights that mark Louisiana's navigable lakes and bayous, the New Canal Lighthouse stands on the banks of Lake Pontchartrain, several miles north of downtown New Orleans. The lighthouse took its name from an ambitious, though failed, canal-building project begun during the early 1830s. Although the so-called "New Canal" was intended to link Pontchartrain with the New Orleans business district and with the Mississippi River, it was never completed. But while construction continued, a small, bustling harbor developed at the canal's terminus on Lake Pontchartrain.

In 1834 Congress provided $25,000, a considerable sum at that time, for a lighthouse to guide lake traffic in and out of the harbor. The lighthouse was probably made of brick, but despite that and its relatively high cost, it deteriorated rapidly. By 1854 the structure was considered unrepairable and had to be demolished.

It was soon replaced by a cottage-style lighthouse consisting of a lantern on the roof of a keeper's dwelling. Built for only $6,000, this new lighthouse survived the Civil War and remained in service for more than three decades.

The board discontinued the lighthouse in 1890 and sold the building at public auction. For more than a year the harbor was marked by a lantern hung from a high pole. Meanwhile, workmen erected the two-story, white-frame lighthouse that still stands beside the lake.

Today, only a few traces of the New Canal can be seen, but the lighthouse that bears its name remains active. The building that once doubled as a keeper's dwelling and lighthouse now serves as headquarters for the Coast Guard's Lake Pontchartrain rescue service.

Take I-10 and I-610 to the West End Boulevard North exit. Then take West End Boulevard to Lake Shore Boulevard and Lake Pontchartrain. The lighthouse is visible from Lake Shore Boulevard. Tours can be arranged with the Coast Guard by calling (504) 589–2331 on the same day you want to visit.

The new Canal Light on Lake Pontchartrain has been active since 1838.

BOLIVAR POINT LIGHT
Near Galveston, Texas - 1852

Built in 1852, the original Bolivar Point Light was constructed of cast-iron sections that raised the lantern more than 100 feet above sea level. When the Civil War broke out, the Confederates pulled down the tower and reforged the iron, apparently using it to make weapons. Reconstruction of the lighthouse following the war was cut short by a yellow-fever epidemic that caused the government to place several hundred miles of the Texas coast under quarantine.

The new lighthouse, erected at a cost of more than $50,000 by work crews brought in from New Orleans, was not completed until late 1872. Like its predecessor and the lighthouse at Biloxi, the tower had an iron shell. This greatly increased the strength of the tower, enabling it to survive numerous gales, such as the disastrous hurricane in 1900 (described in the introduction to this chapter).

In 1915 another hurricane bore down on Galveston, and once more, the Bolivar Point Lighthouse became a refuge. This time about sixty people climbed onto the tower steps to escape the wind and the flood tide accompanying the storm. The flood carried away the tank containing the oil supply for the lamps so that the light was extinguished for two critical days following the storm.

Discontinued by the Coast Guard in 1933, the Bolivar Point Light has been dark now for more than half a century.

Now privately owned and closed to the public, the tower can be seen from State 87 on the Bolivar Peninsula. To reach the peninsula, take the free ferry from the north end of Galveston Island. The ferry provides an excellent view of the lighthouse.

The Bolivar Point Light survived a severe hurricane on the Gulf of Mexico in 1900.

MATAGORDA LIGHT
Matagorda Island, Texas - 1852

The government built several lighthouses along the Texas coast in 1852, including those at Bolivar Point and Matagorda Bay. The Matagorda Lighthouse had a cast-iron tower much like the one at Bolivar, raising the lens ninety-one feet above the entrance to Matagorda Bay. Sailors had no trouble distinguishing it from other coastal towers since it was painted in red, white, and black horizontal bands.

During the early 1860s, Confederate soldiers stole the lens and apparatus and buried them in the sand. Their attempt to blow up the lighthouse with kegs of gunpowder severely damaged the tower but did not topple it. However, where the rebels failed, erosion and neglect succeeded. In 1867 the tower had to be dismantled to keep it from falling over on its own. The Lighthouse Board then rebuilt the lighthouse some two miles from its original site and had it back in service by 1873.

A powerful storm battered the Matagorda Lighthouse for two days during the late summer of 1886. Wind shook the tower so hard that a piece of the lens fell out and smashed on the floor of the lantern. Except for the tower itself and the keeper's house, wind and water swept away everything. Fortunately, the keeper had the foresight to store twenty gallons of fuel inside the tower, so that he was able to keep the light burning.

The light still burns today, marking the man-made ship channel through Pass Cavallo and into Matagorda Bay. It can be seen by the pilots of ships from as far as twenty-five miles at sea.

This lighthouse can only be reached by charter boat. For more information, contact the Friends of Matagorda Island, Box 1099, Port Lavaca, Texas 77979; (512) 552–2803.

This vintage photograph depicts the Matagorda Lighthouse as it looked in 1914.

POINT ISABEL LIGHT
Point Isabel, Texas - 1852

Also constructed in 1852, a good year for lighthouses in Texas, the Point Isabel Light was erected on an old army camp used by the forces of General Zachary Taylor during the Mexican War. The site also attracted considerable military interest during the Civil War. Both the Confederate and Northern forces used the tower as an observation post, and on May 13, 1865, the two sides fought each other at Palmito Ranch, almost within a rifle shot of the lighthouse. The Southerners won the battle but discovered, to their dismay, that they had already lost the war. Robert E. Lee had surrendered at Appomattox Courthouse in Virginia more than a month earlier.

Sea traffic in the vicinity of Port Isabel began to decline after the war, and in 1888 the Lighthouse Board discontinued the light. A few years later, when board members voted to re-exhibit the light, they were very surprised to learn that the government no longer owned the lighthouse. Technically speaking, the government had never owned Point Isabel itself. It seems that General Taylor had not purchased the land but had illegally expropriated it for the use of his army. After years of litigation and negotiation, the board ended up having to buy back its own lighthouse from a Texas rancher for $6,000.

Shortly after the turn of the century, the Isabel Light fell permanently dark. Although not used for more than eighty years, it remains in excellent condition, the centerpiece, in fact, of Texas's smallest state park.

The lighthouse stands on a hill beside State 100 just east of the junction with State 48 in the center of Port Isabel. The state of Texas maintains the lighthouse. There are self-guided tours daily.

For more information, contact the Texas Parks and Wildlife Department, 4200 Smith School Road, Austin, Texas 78744; (512) 943–1172.

Point Isabel Light has stood for nearly 140 years.

HALFMOON REEF LIGHT
Port Lavaca, Texas - 1858

The Halfmoon Reef Lighthouse once stood on pilings in the middle of Matagorda Bay. Today it sits on land beside the Chamber of Commerce building in Port Lavaca, Texas.

Erected in 1858, the lighthouse warned ships away from the dangerous Halfmoon Reef in Matagorda Bay. Although located over open water, it survived countless storms, including major hurricanes in 1864, 1875, and 1886. It took a truly calamitous hurricane in 1942 to put it out of service.

The following year, the lighthouse narrowly missed being blown to bits by a flight of World War II bombers. A crew had just arrived to load the sagging structure onto a barge—it had been knocked off its pilings by the hurricane—and move it to land. The crew was still hard at work when a Coast Guard vessel pulled alongside with some alarming news. In less than thirty minutes the area was scheduled for use as a bombing range. Luckily, the Coast Guard managed to wave off the airplanes before they dropped their explosives.

For many years, the Halfmoon Reef Lighthouse sat dilapidated and abandoned at the Point Comfort dredging yard. But in 1979 it was moved overland to Port Lavaca where, instead of a coastal mark, it is now a landmark.

Originally located in Matagorda Bay at the tip of Halfmoon Reef, the lighthouse now stands on State 35 at Port Lavaca. For more information, contact the Port Lavaca-Calhoun County Chamber of Commerce (located next door to the lighthouse), Box 528, Port Lavaca, Texas 77979.

The Halfmoon Reef Light now stands on land in Port Lavaca, Texas.

BIBLIOGRAPHY

Adams, William Henry Davenport. *Lighthouses and Lightships: A Descriptive and Historical Account of Their Mode of Construction and Organization.* New York: Scribner's, 1870.

Adamson, Hans Christian. *Keepers of the Light.* New York: Greenberg, 1955.

Beaver, Patrick. *A History of Lighthouses.* Secaucus, N.J.: Citadel, 1972.

Buehr, Walter. *Storm Warning: The Story of Hurricanes and Tornadoes.* New York: Morrow, 1972.

Chase, Mary Ellen. *The Story of Lighthouses.* New York: Norton, 1965.

Cipra, David L. *Lighthouses and Lightships of the Gulf of Mexico.* U.S. Coast Guard, 1978.

Conway, Martin. *The Outer Banks: An Historical Adventure from Kitty Hawk to Ocracoke.* Shepherdstown, W.V.: Carabelle Books, 1985.

Dean, Love. *Reef Lights: Seaswept Lighthouses of the Florida Keys.* Key West: The Historic Key West Preservation Board, 1982.

DuBois, Bessie Wilson. "Jupiter Lighthouse."*The Journal of the Historical Association of Southern Florida* 20 (1960).

de Gast, Robert. *The Lighthouses of the Chesapeake.* Baltimore: Johns Hopkins University, 1973.

Holland, Francis Ross, Jr. *America's Lighthouses: Their Illustrated History Since 1716.* Brattleboro, Vt.: Stephen Greene Press, 1972.

Kagerer, Rudy. *A Guidebook to Lighthouses: In South Carolina, Georgia, and Florida's East Coast.* Athens, Ga.: Lighthouse Enterprises, 1985.

Marx, Robert. *Shipwrecks of the Western Hemisphere.* New York: David McKay Company, 1971.

Mason, Herbert Mollow. *Death from the Seas: The Galveston Hurricane of 1900.* New York: Dial, 1972.

McCormick, William Henry. *The Modern Book of Lighthouses, Lifeboats, and Lightships.* London: W. Heinemann, 1913.

Moe, Christine. *Lighthouses and Lightships.* Monticello, Ill.: 1979.

Naush, John M. *Seamarks: Their History and Development.* London: Stanford Maritime, 1985.

Parker, Tony. *Lighthouse.* New York: Taplinger, 1976.

Pouliot, Richard, and Julie Pouliot. *Shipwrecks on the Virginia Coast.* Centreville, Md.: Tidewater, 1986.

Scheina, Robert L. "The Evolution of the Lighthouse Tower," *Lighthouses: Then and Now* (supplement to the U.S. Coast Guard Commandant's Bulletin).

Shomette, Donald. *Shipwrecks on the Chesapeake.* Centreville, Md.: Tidewater, 1982.

Simpson, Robert. *The Hurricane and Its Impact.* Baton Rouge: Louisiana State University, 1980.

Snowe, Edward Rowe, *Famous Lighthouses of America.* New York: Dodd, Mead, 1955.

———— *Great Gales and Dire Disasters.* New York: Dodd, Mead, 1952.

Stick, David. *North Carolina Lighthouses.* (Raleigh, N.C.: North Carolina Department of Cultural Resources, 1980.

Talbot, Frederick Arthur Ambrose. *Lightships and Lighthouses.* London: W. Heinemann, 1913.

Tate, Suzanne. *Whalehead: Tales of Corolla, N.C.* Nags Head, N.C.: Nags Head Art, 1987.

United States Coast Guard. *Historically Famous Lighthouses.* CG-232, 1986.

———— *Chronology of Aids to Navigation and the Old Lighthouse Service.* CG 458, 1974.

Weiss, George. *The Lighthouse Service: Its History, Activities and Organization.* Baltimore: Johns Hopkins University, 1926.

Witney, Dudley. *The Lighthouse.* Boston: New York Graphic Society, 1975.

ABOUT THE AUTHORS

BRUCE ROBERTS is a senior photographer for *Southern Living* magazine and lives in Birmingham, Albama. He started his career working on newspapers in Tampa, Florida; Wilmington, Delaware; and Charlotte, North Carolina. His award-winning photographs have appeared in *Life, Sports Illustrated,* Time-Life Books, and other magazines and books; some rest in the permanent collection of the Smithsonian Institution. Both the Georgia and national nature conservancies have reprinted Bruce's nature photography.

RAY JONES is a freelance writer living in Washington, D.C. He has been a text editor for Time-Life Books, an editor at *Albuquerque Living,* and a writing coach and senior editor at *Southern Living* magazine. Mr. Jones grew up in Macon, Georgia, was inspired by the writing of Faulkner and Hemingway, and worked his way through college as a disc jockey. He holds a B.A. in history and political science and has completed postgraduate work in literature, nonfiction writing, and philosophy.